ALCOHOL AND DRUG ABUSE

DRUG-IMPAIRED DRIVING

DATA AND REDUCTION STRATEGIES

ALCOHOL AND DRUG ABUSE

Additional books in this series can be found on Nova's website under the Series tab.

Additional e-books in this series can be found on Nova's website under the e-book tab.

CONTENTS

Preface		**vii**
Chapter 1	Drug-Impaired Driving: Additional Support Needed for Public Awareness Initiatives *United States Government Accountability Office*	**1**
Chapter 2	Drug and Alcohol Crash Risk *Richard P. Compton and Amy Berning*	**39**
Chapter 3	Results of the 2013–2014 National Roadside Survey of Alcohol and Drug Use by Drivers *Amy Berning, Richard Compton and Kathryn Wochinger*	**63**
Chapter 3	Drug-Impaired Driving: Understanding the Problem and Ways to Reduce It *R. Compton, M. Vegega and D. Smither*	**75**
Index		**103**

PREFACE

This book discusses what is known about the extent of drug-impaired driving in the United States; challenges that exist for federal, state, and local agencies in addressing drug-impaired driving; and actions federal and state agencies have taken to address drug-impaired driving and what gaps exist in the federal response. This book also summarizes a series of studies undertaken by the National Highway Traffic Safety Administration to acquire the information needed to address the general problem of drug-impaired driving.

Chapter 1 – The issue of alcohol-impaired driving has received broad attention over the years, but drug-impaired driving also contributes to fatalities and injuries from traffic crashes. However, knowledge about the drug-impaired- driving problem is less advanced than for alcohol-impaired driving. Through Senate Report No. 113-45 (2013), Congress required GAO to report on the strategies NHTSA, ONDCP, and states have taken to address drug-impaired driving and challenges they face in detecting and reducing such driving. This report discusses (1) what is known about the extent of drug-impaired driving in the United States; (2) challenges that exist for federal, state, and local agencies in addressing drug-impaired driving; and (3) actions federal and state agencies have taken to address drug-impaired driving and what gaps exist in the federal response. GAO reviewed literature to identify sources of data on drug-impaired driving; reviewed documentation and interviewed officials from NHTSA, ONDCP, and HHS; and interviewed officials from relevant advocacy and professional organizations and seven selected states. States were selected based on: legal status of marijuana, proximity to states with legalized marijuana, and drugged-driving laws.

Chapter 2 – While the extent of use of alcohol by drivers and the risks posed by alcohol use have been well known for many decades, relatively little has been known about the use of other drugs by drivers and the associated risks. However, drug-impaired driving has recently become an issue of increasing public and governmental concern in the United States and in many other countries (Compton et al., 2009; Asbridge et al., 2012; ICADTS, 2007). While it is readily apparent that driving-related skills can be impaired by a wide variety of illegal substances and medications, the nature and scope of the drug-impaired driving problem has been difficult to define (Jones et al., 2003; DuPont et al., 2012; Houwing, 2013). In the United States, recent State actions to legalize the use of marijuana for medical and recreational use have further exacerbated concern over potential risks of driving impaired by marijuana. Marijuana is the most frequently detected drug (other than alcohol) in crash-involved drivers as well as the general driving population (Terhune, 1982; Terhune et al., 1992; Lacey et al., 2009; Walsh et al., 2005). There is evidence that marijuana use impairs psychomotor skills, divided attention, lane tracking, and cognitive functions (Robbe et al., 1993; Moskowitz, 1995; Hartman and Huestis, 2013). However, its role in contributing to the occurrence of crashes remains less clear. Many studies, using a variety of methods have attempted to estimate the risk of driving after use of marijuana (Li et al., 2012; Asbridge et al., 2012). The methods have included experimental studies, observational studies, and epidemiological studies. While useful in identifying how marijuana affects the performance of driving tasks, experimental and observational studies do not lend themselves to predicting real world crash risk.

Chapter 3 – Over the last four decades, the National Highway Traffic Safety Administration and/or the Insurance Institute for Highway Safety (IIHS) conducted four national surveys to estimate the prevalence of drinking and driving in the United States (Wolfe, 1974; Lund & Wolfe, 1991; Voas et al, 1998; Compton & Berning, 2009; Lacey et al, 2009). The first National Roadside Survey (NRS) was conducted in 1973, followed by national surveys of drivers in 1986, 1996, 2007, and now 2013–2014. These surveys used a stratified random sample of weekend nighttime drivers in the contiguous 48 States and collected data directly from drivers on the road.

Chapter 4 – This report was prepared in accordance with Section 2013 of the Safe, Accountable, Flexible, Efficient Transportation Equity Act: A Legacy for Users (SAFETEA-LU). The report summarizes a series of studies undertaken by the National Highway Traffic Safety Administration to acquire the information needed to address the general problem of drug-impaired driving. The report describes the research conducted on prevention, detection, and prosecution of driving under the influence of drugs; issues associated with determining what drugs impair driving; difficulties in relating blood levels of drugs and impairment; lack of information about what drugs are frequently used by drivers and what drugs elevate crash risk; problems in obtaining representative data about current enforcement, prosecution, and adjudication of drug-impaired driving; training for law enforcement officers in recognizing drug-impaired drivers; review of drug-impaired driving laws; and what is known about the role of drugs as causal factors in traffic crashes. It highlights the need for further research and concludes with recommendations to better address the problem of drug-impaired driving.

In: Drug-Impaired Driving
Editor: Tobias H. Erickson
ISBN: 978-1-63482-871-0

Chapter 1

DRUG-IMPAIRED DRIVING: ADDITIONAL SUPPORT NEEDED FOR PUBLIC AWARENESS INITIATIVES*

United States Government Accountability Office

WHY GAO DID THIS STUDY

The issue of alcohol-impaired driving has received broad attention over the years, but drug-impaired driving also contributes to fatalities and injuries from traffic crashes. However, knowledge about the drug-impaired- driving problem is less advanced than for alcohol-impaired driving.

Through Senate Report No. 113-45 (2013), Congress required GAO to report on the strategies NHTSA, ONDCP, and states have taken to address drug-impaired driving and challenges they face in detecting and reducing such driving. This report discusses (1) what is known about the extent of drug-impaired driving in the United States; (2) challenges that exist for federal, state, and local agencies in addressing drug-impaired driving; and (3) actions federal and state agencies have taken to address drug-impaired driving and what gaps exist in the federal response. GAO reviewed literature to identify sources of data on drug-impaired driving; reviewed documentation and interviewed officials from NHTSA, ONDCP, and HHS; and interviewed

* This is an edited, reformatted and augmented version of a United States Government Accountability Office publication, No. GAO-15-293, dated February 2015.

officials from relevant advocacy and professional organizations and seven selected states. States were selected based on: legal status of marijuana, proximity to states with legalized marijuana, and drugged-driving laws.

What GAO Recommends

GAO recommends that NHTSA take additional actions to support states in emphasizing to the public the dangers of drug-impaired driving. DOT agreed with GAO's recommendation.

What GAO Found

Various state and national-level data sources—including surveys, arrest data, drug-testing results, and crash data—provide limited information on the extent of drugged and drug-impaired driving in the United States. For example, based on preliminary results from a representative sample of weekend-nighttime and Friday daytime drivers, the National Highway Traffic Safety Administration's (NHTSA) *2013-2014 National Roadside Survey of Alcohol and Drug Use by Drivers* (*NRS*) estimated that 20 percent of drivers would have tested positive for at least one drug, with marijuana being the most common drug. However, the survey does not capture the extent to which drivers were impaired by drugs. Arrest data and drug-testing results provide some information on drug-impaired driving, but these data are limited. For example, data for drug impairment may not be separated from that for alcohol impairment and drug testing is not standardized. According to NHTSA officials, currently available data on drug involvement in crashes are generally unreliable due to variances in reporting and testing.

The lack of a clear link between impairment and drug concentrations in the body makes it difficult to define drug impairment, which, in turn, exacerbates challenges related to enforcement and public awareness. Compared to alcohol, defining and identifying impairment due to drugs is more complicated due to the large number of available drugs and their unpredictable effects. For example, the *NRS* includes tests for 75 illegal prescriptions, and over-the-counter (OTC) drugs identified as potentially impairing. Additionally, law enforcement processes for obtaining samples for drug testing can be time consuming and result in a loss of evidence. For example, there is no validated device for roadside drug testing, and obtaining a search warrant to collect a blood sample to confirm the presence of drugs in a driver's system could take several hours, during which time the concentration of the drug in the driver's system could dissipate. Further, state officials identified limited public awareness about the dangers of drugged driving as a challenge. As a result, members of the public may drive while impaired without knowing the risks, potentially leading to collisions, injuries, and fatalities.

Federal and state agencies—including NHTSA, the White House Office of National Drug Control Policy (ONDCP), and the Department of Health and Human Services (HHS)—are taking actions to address drug-impaired driving, including improvements in the areas of research and data, education for police officers, evidence gathering, and legal changes. For example, NHTSA is currently conducting research to assess the crash risk associated with drug use (including illegal, prescription, and OTC drugs) by collecting samples from more than 10,000 drivers. However, public awareness of the dangers of drug-impaired driving is an area in which state officials told us that NHTSA could do more to support their efforts. As part of its mission to support state safety efforts, NHTSA has provided media and other materials to states for impaired-driving awareness programs, but these materials are focused on alcohol-impaired driving. While NHTSA plans to improve public awareness through initiatives to conduct surveys on drug-impaired-driving behaviors and attitudes as well as training for medical professionals, these plans could take several years to implement. Additional efforts, such as general messaging reminding the public about the impairing effects of drugs, could help improve public awareness in the near term.

ABBREVIATIONS

ARIDE	Advanced Roadside Impaired Driving Enforcement
BAC	blood-alcohol concentration
CDC	Centers for Disease Control and Prevention
DOJ	Department of Justice
DRE	Drug Recognition Expert
DUI	driving under the influence of alcohol and/or drugs
DUID	driving under the influence of drugs
FARS	Fatality Analysis Reporting System
FDA	Food and Drug Administration

GHSA	Governors Highway Safety Association
HHS	Department of Health and Human Services
IACP	International Association of Chiefs of Police
JOL	Judicial Outreach Liaison
MADD	Mothers Against Drunk Driving
MAP-21	Moving Ahead for Progress in the 21st Century Act
NCSL	National Conference of State Legislatures
NHTSA	National Highway Traffic Safety Administration
NIDA	National Institute on Drug Abuse
NIH	National Institutes of Health
NRS	*National Roadside Survey of Alcohol and Drug Use by Drivers*
NSDUH	National Survey on Drug Use and Health
NTSB	National Transportation Safety Board
ONDCP	Office of National Drug Control Policy
OTC	over-the-counter
PIRE	Pacific Institute for Research and Evaluation
SAMHSA	Substance Abuse and Mental Health Services Administration
SOFT	Society of Forensic Toxicologists, Inc.
THC	tetrahydrocannabinol
TSRP	Traffic Safety Resource Prosecutor

* * *

February 24, 2015

The Honorable Susan Collins
Chairman
The Honorable Jack Reed
Ranking Member
Subcommittee on Transportation,
Housing and Urban Development, and
Related Agencies
Committee on Appropriations
United States Senate

The Honorable Mario Diaz-Balart
Chairman
The Honorable David Price

Ranking Member
Subcommittee on Transportation,
Housing and Urban Development, and
Related Agencies
Committee on Appropriations
House of Representatives

While the issue of alcohol-impaired driving has received broad attention over the years, drug-impaired driving also contributes to fatalities and injuries from traffic crashes. However, knowledge about the nature of the drug-impaired driving problem is significantly less advanced than for alcohol-impaired driving. Based on preliminary results from a nationally representative sample in 2013-2014, an estimated 20 percent of nighttime weekend drivers would have tested positive for illegal, prescription, or over-the-counter (OTC) drugs that have been identified as potentially impairing.[1] The White House's Office of National Drug Control Policy (ONDCP) has identified "drugged driving" as a policy priority, and established a goal in the agency's 2011 National Drug Control Strategy to reduce drugged driving 10 percent by 2015.[2] The National Highway Traffic Safety Administration (NHTSA) assists states in implementing programs to address impaired driving—including those aimed at reducing drug-impaired driving—and has funded research examining the extent and nature of drug-impaired driving as well as the effectiveness of countermeasures.

The Senate Report accompanying the Transportation and Housing and Urban Development, and Related Agencies Appropriations Bill, 2014 required GAO to report on the strategies that NHTSA, ONDCP, and states have taken to address drug impairment and the challenges faced in detecting and reducing drug-impaired driving. 3 This report discusses (1) what is known about the extent of drug-impaired driving in the United States; (2) challenges that exist for federal, state, and local agencies in addressing drug-impaired driving; and (3) actions federal and state agencies have taken to address drug-impaired driving and gaps that exist in the federal response to drug-impaired driving.

This report uses the term "drug-impaired driving" to refer to driving while impaired by illegal drugs or prescription and OTC (legal) medications. For this work, we conducted a literature search to identify sources of data and studies on the issue and extent of drug-impaired driving, reviewed these data and studies, and determined their limitations. Additionally, we reviewed documentation and interviewed officials from seven federal agencies:

NHTSA; ONDCP; National Transportation Safety Board (NTSB); Department of Health and Human Services (HHS) and component agencies including the Substance Abuse and Mental Health Services Administration (SAMHSA), Centers for Disease Control and Prevention (CDC), Food and Drug Administration (FDA), and National Institutes of Health (NIH). 4 We also reviewed documentation obtained from and interviewed officials with responsibilities related to drug-impaired driving, such as traffic safety, toxicology lab, and law enforcement officials, in seven states (Arizona, California, Colorado, Kansas, Ohio, Vermont, and Washington). We selected these states based on recommendations from federal officials and representatives from advocacy and professional organizations and to represent a variety of laws, programs, and other factors. Our selection included:

- states with legalized recreational marijuana,
- states that geographically border states in which recreational marijuana use is legal,
- states with legalized medical marijuana,
- states representing a variety of drug-impaired driving laws, and
- states identified as having robust programs dealing with driving under the influence of drugs.

We also reviewed documentation and interviewed representatives from advocacy and professional organizations, including the Governors Highway Safety Association (GHSA), National District Attorneys Association, Society of Forensic Toxicologists, Inc. (SOFT), Mothers Against Drunk Driving (MADD), International Association of Chiefs of Police (IACP), Insurance Institute for Highway Safety, and National Conference of State Legislatures (NCSL). See additional information on our scope and methodology in appendix I.

We conducted this performance audit from April 2014 through February 2015 in accordance with generally accepted government auditing standards. Those standards require that we plan and perform the audit to obtain sufficient, appropriate evidence to provide a reasonable basis for our findings and conclusions based on our audit objectives. We believe the evidence obtained provides a reasonable basis for our findings and conclusions based on our audit objectives.

BACKGROUND

Similar to drunk driving, drug-impaired driving can result in crashes leading to death or injury of vehicle occupants and pedestrians, along with other safety and traffic issues for individuals and society. Taking into consideration these possible harms, Congress has authorized grant funding to states to combat impaired driving through transportation legislation—most recently the Moving Ahead for Progress in the 21st Century Act (MAP-21).[5] These grant programs are designed to encourage states to adopt and implement effective programs to reduce driving under the influence of alcohol, drugs, or the combination of alcohol and drugs. Historically, these programs have been focused on reducing alcohol-impaired driving. For example, in the late 1990s, Congress made grant funds available to states to encourage them to lower the illegal per se driving blood-alcohol concentration (BAC) limit to 0.08.[6] In other words, with respect to a BAC limit of 0.08, anyone whose blood contains 8/100th of 1 percent of alcohol (or higher) would be deemed to be driving while intoxicated. All 50 states and the District of Columbia have 0.08 laws as well as laws making it illegal to drive while impaired by drugs.

NHTSA administers grant programs for safety initiatives to assist states in their efforts to reduce traffic-related fatalities, including fatalities involving drug- and alcohol-impaired driving. NHTSA also provides guidance and technical assistance to states, and conducts research on drivers' behavior and traffic safety. As part of such research, NHTSA works with traffic safety organizations, such as GHSA and MADD, and other federal agencies, such as ONDCP. In addition to NHTSA, other federal agencies conduct research and implement programs that, in whole or in part, seek to increase knowledge about the problem of drug-impaired driving and to identify and implement policies and programs to reduce drug-impaired driving. These agencies include ONDCP; HHS's SAMHSA, NIH, FDA, and CDC; Department of Justice (DOJ); and NTSB.

Drug-impaired driving may be caused by use of illegal drugs, legally prescribed or OTC drugs that are misused, and some legally prescribed or OTC drugs even when used as intended.[7] While 23 states and the District of Columbia have legalized the use of marijuana for medical purposes, according to the NCSL, and two states—Colorado and Washington—allow the use of marijuana for recreational purposes, the federal government continues to consider marijuana as an illegal drug, with no medical use.[8] Throughout the report, we have noted instances in which data may include marijuana as either a legal or illegal drug. According to the FDA, some prescription and OTC drugs can impair driving ability, while others have no effect or can even enable patients to drive more safely.

For the purposes of this report, we have used the following terminology:

- **Drugged driving:** driving with the presence of drugs in one's system regardless of impairment.
- **Drug-impaired driving:** driving with a diminished ability to operate a vehicle due to drug use.
- **Drug test:** the toxicological analysis of a biological specimen—blood, urine, or oral fluid (saliva)—to determine the presence or absence of specific drugs or their metabolites.
- **DUI:** driving under the influence of alcohol and/or drugs.
- **DUID:** driving under the influence of drugs.
- **Impairment:** a diminished ability to perform specific functions.
- **Metabolites:** the products of drug metabolism found in bodily fluids, which indicate prior drug use.
- **Tetrahydrocannabinol (THC):** the main psychoactive compound found in the cannabis (marijuana) plant.
- **Toxicology:** the study of the effects of drugs—whether illegal, prescription, or over-the-counter—on humans.

Drugs may be categorized in several ways including by the chemical type or by the way the drug is used. For example, this report uses the following terms to classify drugs, among others:

- **Antidepressants:** drugs used to treat depression and other conditions, including anxiety disorders.
- **Cannabinoids:** compounds contained in marijuana.
- **Narcotics:** drugs including opium and those derived from it, such as heroin and codeine.
- **Depressants:** drugs that inhibit the activity of the brain and may result in muscle relaxation, lowered blood pressure and heart rate, and slowed breathing; includes anxiety and seizure medications.
- **Stimulants:** drugs that may result in increased alertness and elevated heart rate and respiration; includes cocaine and amphetamines.
- **Synthetics:** synthetic drugs, as opposed to natural drugs such as marijuana, are chemically produced in a laboratory to mimic the effects of other drugs. Synthetic drugs may be developed in order to

circumvent existing drug laws. Examples include synthetic cannabinoids and cathinones.

Limited Data Exists on the Extent of Drug-Impaired Driving in the U.S.

There is no national source of data on the extent of drug-impaired driving in the United States, but various state and national sources of data on drugged driving can provide limited information on the extent to which drivers in the United States have drugs in their systems. For example, national and state roadside surveys provide information on the prevalence of drugged driving in respective survey areas. Other sources of data provide some information on drugged and drug-impaired driving, such as surveys on self-reported drugged-driving behavior, impaired- driving arrests and toxicology results, and crash data.[9] However, limitations to the currently available data include underreporting and a lack of centralization or standardization in reporting.

Survey Data on Prevalence of Drugged Driving

National and state roadside surveys provide data on the prevalence of drugged driving in statistically representative samples of drivers. For example, NHTSA's 2007 *National Roadside Survey of Alcohol and Drug Use by Drivers* (*NRS*) provides information on drivers testing positive for illegal, prescription, and OTC drugs in a nationally representative sample of weekend-nighttime and Friday daytime drivers.[10] Based on the 2007 survey, NHTSA estimated that 16.3 percent of nighttime drivers nationwide would have tested positive for at least one drug, with marijuana being the most common drug found in test results (see table 1). While *NRS* survey data provides useful information on the estimated prevalence of drugged driving, these results do not measure the extent to which drivers are impaired by the drugs in their systems as the presence of drugs or drug metabolites does not necessarily indicate impairment. For example, marijuana metabolites can be detected in blood samples several weeks after daily users' last use. Nonetheless, the 2007 *NRS* provided the first objective data on drug use among drivers in the United States and, according to officials at the National Institute on Drug Abuse (NIDA) and SOFT, served as a wake-up call regarding the extent of drugged-driving in the United States. According to NHTSA, the survey was repeated in 2013-2014 following the same general methodology as the 2007 survey and results will be available in 2015. Preliminary results from that survey estimated that 20 percent of nighttime weekend drivers would have tested positive for illegal, prescription, or OTC drugs that have been identified as potentially impairing.[11] An assessment of trends in drugged driving in the United States may be feasible as future results beyond the 2013-2014 *NRS* become available. Table 1 shows additional drug test results from this survey.

Table 1. Most Common Drugs Found in Test Results for Drivers, 2007 and 2012

	2007 ***National Roadside Survey***[a]	**2012** ***California Roadside Survey***[b]
Marijuana	6.8%	5.5%
Stimulants	3.2%	3.2%
Poly-Use (more than one class of drug)	2.8%	3%
Narcotic-Analgesics	1.6%	1.1%
Sedatives	0.8%	0.7%
Antidepressants	0.7%	0.2%
Other	0.3%	0.3%
Total	**16.3%**	**14%**

Sources: National Highway Traffic Safety Administration's (NHTSA*) 2007 National Roadside Survey of Alcohol and Drug Use by Drivers: Drug Results* (*NRS*) and Results of the 2012 California Roadside Survey of Nighttime Weekend Drivers' Alcohol and Drug Use. | GAO-15-293

[a]During daytime Friday times, drivers were tested for the presence of drugs using oral fluid. During nighttime weekend times, drivers were tested for the presence of drugs using oral fluid and blood. A positive test for either oral fluid or blood is a positive drug test.

[b]During nighttime weekend times, drivers were tested for the presence of drugs using oral fluid. A positive oral fluid test is a positive drug test.

California's Office of Traffic Safety found results similar to the 2007 *NRS* during its 2012 *California Roadside Survey of Nighttime Weekend Drivers' Alcohol and Drug Use* (see table 1).[12] Specifically, 14 percent of nighttime weekend drivers tested positive for at least one drug, with marijuana being the most frequent drug identified. Additionally, the Washington Traffic Safety Commission has commissioned the first of two roadside surveys, using what NHTSA describes as comparable methodology to the 2007 *NRS*, meant to measure drug and alcohol use among drivers before and after implementation of the 2012 state law legalizing recreational marijuana use. Results from the survey are expected in 2015.

Surveys on Drug Use Behavior

The *NRS* and California surveys also collected self-reported data on drug use among drivers who participated in the survey.[13] For instance, during the *California Survey*, approximately 14 percent of all drivers who reported having used marijuana in the past reported having used it within 2 hours of driving in the past year. In the *NRS*, all drivers who provided an oral fluid sample were asked to report if they had used a drug before driving and, if so, what type. For the subset of Friday and nighttime weekend drivers who tested positive for at least one drug based on the oral fluid sample, the drivers' answers regarding prior drug use were compared to positive oral fluid-analysis results to determine agreement between self-reported behavior and the oral fluid test. Results of this comparison include:

- an estimated 7.5 percent of nighttime weekend drivers testing positive for cocaine reported they had used cocaine in the past 24 hours,
- an estimated 25.7 percent of nighttime weekend drivers testing positive for marijuana reported they had used marijuana in the past 24 hours,
- an estimated 59.9 percent of nighttime weekend drivers testing positive for pain medication reported they had used pain medication in the past 24 hours, and
- an estimated 66.4 percent of nighttime weekend drivers testing positive for antidepressants reported they had used antidepressants in the past 24 hours.

Agreement between reported drug use in the past 24 hours and positive oral-fluid-analysis results for the nighttime-driving samples was greatest among users of antidepressants, cough suppressants, and pain medications and lowest for amphetamines and barbiturates.[14] While self-reported data may be useful in tracking trends in reported drug use and attitudes about drugged driving, the *NRS* methodology noted that it may under-report actual activity and therefore be insufficient for estimating the extent of drugged driving.

Additional studies compile self-reported data on attitudes and behaviors regarding drug use and driving, which may be helpful in tracking trends in behavior. SAMHSA's National Survey on Drug Use and Health (NSDUH) is an annual survey of a nationally representative sample of the United States population.[15] The NSDUH includes questions specific to driving while under the influence of illegal drugs. According to this survey, driving under the influence of illegal drugs is most common in respondents aged 18–25 (an estimated 10.6 percent in 2013, the latest survey results available). Overall, the percentage of respondents aged 12 or older who report driving under the influence of illegal drugs in the past year has been around 4 percent from 2008 through 2012.[16] NIH's NIDA also supports various studies on drug use including the College Life Study on health-related behaviors of college students, and Monitoring the Future, which measures attitudes of adolescents related to drug and alcohol use.[17] According to the 2012 Monitoring the Future Survey, an estimated 10.6 percent of high school seniors drove a car, truck, or motorcycle in the prior 2 weeks after having smoked marijuana.[18]

Data on Impaired-Driving Arrests and Toxicology Results

Data on drug-impaired driving arrests and toxicology results in our seven selected states provide some information on drug-impaired driving, but are limited by a lack of separation of data from driving under the influence (DUI) arrests, underreported instances of drug-impaired driving, decentralized reporting, and a lack of standardization in drug testing. For example, officials in six of the seven selected states told us that state arrest data does not currently separate data on drug-impaired driving and alcohol-impaired driving cases across law enforcement agencies. Officials from California stated that although the state recently revised its vehicle code to delineate DUI into three separate reportable sections, it could be several years until any data generated from the new system can be considered complete and accurate.[19] Arizona's Governor's Office of Highway Safety tracks arrests for driving under the influence of alcohol and drugs separately, and data show an increase in drug-impaired driving arrests in the past 5 years, but this rise does not necessarily indicate an increase in drug-impaired driving. For example, Arizona data show a 966 percent increase in drug-impaired driving arrests from 2005 through 2013. However, the increase in arrests may be due to the 659 percent increase in the number of officers participating in impaired-driving enforcement activities, the 1,604 percent increase in the number of traffic stops, and better reporting of those traffic stops, rather than an increase in drug-impaired driving. The rates of contacts resulting in DUID arrests do not show an increasing trend. See table 2.

Table 2. Impaired-Driving Enforcement in Arizona, 2005–2013

	2005	2006	2007	2008	2009	2010	2011	2012	2013
Contacts (All traffic stops)	49,230	72,057	112,555	96,243	148,063	228,146	702,921	877,617	838,979
DUI alcohol arrests	6,501	6,847	10,133	10,409	14,154	19,482	31,561	32,174	31,891
DUI drug arrests	424	541	538	694	1,153	1,679	3,579	4,511	4,519
Officers working on DUI enforcement activities[a]	6,081	6,522	11,483	10,225	15,809	34,300	47,927	51,654	46,139
Contacts that result in DUI drug arrests	.86%	.75%	.47%	.72%	.78%	.74%	.51%	.51%	.54%

Source: GAO analysis of Arizona Governor's Office of Highway Safety data. | GAO-15-293

[a]Officers working on DUI enforcement activities is a cumulative figure: these numbers do not necessarily represent unique officers.

Note: Driving under the influence of alcohol or drugs is referred to as DUI. This data does not include impaired driving enforcement conducted by a small number (about 2 percent) of agencies that do not submit data.

In addition, drug-impaired driving may be underreported as drivers impaired by both alcohol and drugs will likely be tested and prosecuted only for alcohol impairment because, according to officials from NHTSA and six of the seven selected states, evidence collection and prosecution are much easier for alcohol-impaired driving. Officials from NHTSA and six states said that in general, if a person suspected of impaired driving has a BAC over 0.08, the individual is not tested further for the presence of drugs, regardless of whether drug impairment is also suspected. As a result, drivers impaired by both drugs and alcohol may not be reported accurately in arrest data, contributing to a lack of knowledge about the number of drivers impaired by both drugs and alcohol.

Further, based on our review of information from the seven selected states on arrests and toxicology results for DUID cases, we found that state data on impaired driving are often not centralized or complete. Among the selected states, data on DUID arrests are generally collected by local law enforcement agencies, and one of the seven selected states collects statewide data on DUIDs in a centralized database. While Arizona collects arrest data from a majority of its local law enforcement agencies in a central database, a small number of local agencies do not participate. One official estimated about 2 percent of agencies do not submit data. Similarly, statewide toxicology/drug-testing data may not be easily available because it is decentralized. In five of the seven selected states, toxicology data are maintained by individual state and local law enforcement agencies and toxicology labs (including private and public labs), with no centralized database. For example in California, DUID testing varies by jurisdiction and can be completed by one of 22 private labs or 6 public labs at the local or state level. In contrast, Vermont and Washington have centralized results of all DUID drug tests, which are conducted by a single laboratory for each state. While Vermont toxicology data do not show any clear trends, a study using Washington state toxicology data indicates that the prevalence of marijuana in suspected impaired-driving cases increased after marijuana was legalized, from an average of 19.1 percent of cases positive for tetrahydrocannabinol (THC) from 2009 through 2012 to 24.9 percent in 2013 (post legalization).[20] However, according to one of the authors, it is unclear whether this increase is due to factors other than an increase in marijuana-impaired driving, such as an increased focus on marijuana impairment in the state. Over the same period, the prevalence of alcohol and drugs other than marijuana in the population of suspected impaired drivers remained relatively stable in Washington.

Further, drug test results may not be comparable among laboratories. Officials from three of the seven selected states, as well as representatives from SOFT, stated that a lack of standardization among labs means that test results from different labs cannot necessarily be compared. For example, labs do not have uniform reporting-level cutoffs for drugs (the level at which a drug is reported as present). Therefore, for the same sample, one lab may report the sample as positive for the presence of a drug while another lab may report the sample as negative because the amount present is below the reporting level cutoff for the second lab. According to officials from HHS, while there are federal standards for forensic toxicology testing for federal agencies and states may establish standards for forensic testing, there are currently no federal laboratory certification requirements for forensic laboratories conducting toxicology testing for state and local law-enforcement agencies.[21]

Despite these limitations, drug testing results for DUID cases can provide information on the types and amounts of drugs present in drivers' systems. A 2004–2005 survey of labs in the United States conducted by SOFT, in conjunction with the National Safety Council and the American Academy of Forensic Sciences, shows that the most common drug encountered in DUID cases is cannabis (marijuana), followed by benzodiazepines (anti-anxiety medications with sedative properties), then narcotics (including cocaine, hydrocodone, and morphine/codeine).[22] The most common drugs, and how drugs are categorized, differ from region to region, as indicated by toxicological results we gathered from seven state toxicology labs. Four of the selected states do not separate out DUID toxicological testing from other toxicological testing. For the three selected states that have separate toxicology data for DUID cases, the most common drug found for the most recent data available was marijuana; the second most common drug or drug category found was methamphetamine for two states and benzodiazepines in one state.

Federal and State Crash Data

NHTSA and states collect information on drug involvement in fatal crashes, but these data are not complete or consistent, according to NHTSA officials. States collect data on drug involvement in fatal crashes as determined through drug testing of involved drivers, data that then may be reported to NHTSA and aggregated in NHTSA's Fatality Analysis Reporting System (FARS). [23] However, according to NHTSA officials, comparing FARS results from one state to another is problematic because of the limitations and variations in data collection, testing, and reporting noted above, among other things.

DIFFICULTY OF DEFINING DRUG IMPAIRMENT EXACERBATES CHALLENGES RELATED TO ENFORCEMENT AND PUBLIC AWARENESS

In addition to limited data on the extent of drugged and drug-impaired driving, federal and state officials we spoke with cited difficulty in defining drug impairment as a significant challenge to addressing drug-impaired driving. Compared to alcohol, which is chemically simple and has relatively predictable effects, defining and identifying impairment due to drugs is much more complicated due to the large number of available drugs and their unpredictable side effects. The lack of a definition of drug impairment, in turn, exacerbates challenges in enforcing drug-impaired driving laws and informing the public about the dangers of driving under the influence of drugs.

Defining Drug Impairment Is Complex

No Clear Link between Drug Concentration and Impairment

Toxicologists in three of seven selected states, officials from NIDA, SAMSHA, and representatives from SOFT stated that identifying a link between impairment and drug concentrations in the body, similar to the 0.08 BAC threshold established for alcohol, is complex and, according to officials from SOFT, possibly infeasible. Alcohol is a chemically simple molecule that is absorbed and metabolized at a relatively consistent and predictable rate. In contrast, most drugs are chemically complex molecules; various drugs are absorbed and eliminated from an individual's system at different rates. As a result, impairment does not necessarily correspond to a specific concentration level in the blood, and detectable amounts of certain drugs may remain even after impairing effects wear off. For example, as noted earlier, marijuana can be detected in a daily marijuana user's system up to 30 days after using the drug. Toxicologists in four states and representatives from SOFT stated that, as a result, a positive drug test does not necessarily indicate impairment.

Additionally, drugs can have varying and unpredictable effects on individuals. For example, individuals with prescriptions for central nervous system depressants, such as a prescription sleep aid, can develop a tolerance which can reduce some of the impairing effects. During the first few days of taking a prescribed central-nervous-system depressant, a person can feel sleepy and uncoordinated, but as the body becomes accustomed to the effects of the drug and tolerance develops, these side effects begin to disappear. As a result, drug concentrations that would be impairing for one individual may not be impairing to another. Further, drivers may combine more than one drug or mix drugs with alcohol, which can have unpredictable results and cause impairment more quickly than the same amounts of each substance taken alone. According to literature we reviewed, when combined, multiple drugs or drugs and alcohol can have a synergistic effect, rather than a simple additive effect, so each substance may increase the impairing effects of the others.

Analyzing Samples for the Large Number of Available Legal and Illegal Drugs Is Time Consuming and Expensive

Drug testing is more time consuming and expensive than testing for alcohol because rather than the single blood or breath test needed to determine blood alcohol level, separate tests must be conducted for each suspected drug class (e.g., pain relievers, antidepressants), and the required instrumentation is sophisticated and costly.[24] According to toxicologists from two states and representatives from SOFT, it is more expensive to test for drugs than alcohol. For instance, one toxicologist stated that standard equipment for alcohol analysis costs between $100,000 and $120,000; but equipment needed to test for certain types of drugs can cost up to $500,000. Additionally, the number of potentially impairing legal and illegal drugs is large. For example, the *NRS* tested drivers for 75 illegal, prescription, and OTC drugs identified as potentially impairing, and while some medications do not affect or can even improve driving ability, the FDA has identified eight common classes of prescription and OTC medications as potentially impairing.[25] In addition, in 2013, the National Safety Council's Alcohol, Drugs and Impairment Division reviewed and recommended a list of 33 drugs that should be included in the scope of drug testing.[26]

Further, new drugs are continually being developed for both legal and illegal markets, especially synthetics.[27] For instance, the United Nations Office on Drugs and Crime reported that in the United States, 51 synthetic cannabinoids (developed to reproduce the effects of THC/marijuana) and 31 synthetic cathinones (mimicking the effects of amphetamines) were identified in 2012.[28]

According to toxicologists in two states, to pursue detection of new drugs, even if the molecular structure is only slightly different from other known drugs, labs need to develop a new testing methodology and then validate that methodology through extensive testing on each individual instrument. For example, according to one toxicologist, developing and validating testing methods for a new drug recently cost about $31,000. Validation of new methodologies is a complicated task and requires qualified personnel, time, and money. Additionally, one toxicologist stated that, to run tests on synthetic cannabinoids and other synthetics, a standard sample against which to test must be purchased from either a chemical company or another source. The entire process is lengthy and expensive.

Enforcement of DrugImpaired-Driving Laws Is Challenging

Lack of Knowledge among Law Enforcement about Drug Impairment in Drivers

State prosecutors and highway safety office officials in three of the seven selected states said that there is a lack of knowledge among law enforcement about drug impairment in drivers. Furthermore, according to officials from NHTSA, GHSA, and IACP, basic training for officers on impaired driving enforcement is insufficient for identifying drivers that may be impaired by drugs. For example, officers may be trained to administer the Standardized Field Sobriety Test, which focuses on detecting alcohol-impairment in drivers; however, officers may not be trained to recognize drug impairment. One prosecutor stated that there is a misperception among some officers who have not received training to identify drug impairment that a drug-impaired driver should exhibit similar symptoms as a drunken one; including slurred speech and difficulty maintaining balance. As a result, officers who are not trained to detect drug impairment may mistakenly think that a driver is not impaired. See table 3 for a comparison of some of the possible symptoms of alcohol and drug impairment, which vary depending on the type of drug used.

Table 3. Comparison of Examples of Possible Alcohol and Drug-Impairment Symptoms

Alcohol impairment	Depressant impairment	Cocaine impairment	Marijuana impairment
•slurred speech •problems with balance •odor of alcohol on breath	•slurred speech •poor performance on field sobriety tests •drowsiness •disorientation •drunken behavior without the odor of alcohol	•excessive activity •increased alertness •talkativeness •irritability •argumentativeness •nervousness •body tremors •anxiety •redness in nasal area and runny nose	•poor performance on field sobriety tests •odor of marijuana in car oron breath •bloodshot eyes •body and eyelid tremors •incomplete thought processes

Source: National Highway Traffic Safety Administration. | GAO-15-293

Note: This table provides examples of drug impairment symptoms, but does not represent the universe of possible symptoms. Symptoms of drug impairment vary depending on the type of drug used.

Processes for Obtaining Samples for Drug Testing Can Be Time Consuming and Result in Loss of Evidence

The time between arrest and collection of a sample for drug testing can affect the quality of biological evidence, such as blood samples, because the concentration of drugs in the body is constantly changing. Specifically, logistical challenges and legal requirements pertaining to evidence collection can increase the time between arrest and sample collection, reducing evidence quality. Currently, there is no validated roadside drug-testing device, such as the evidential breath-testing device for alcohol, which would facilitate faster sample collection.[29] Drug testing can be conducted from a blood, oral fluid, or urine sample. According to toxicologists from two states, representatives from SOFT, and literature we reviewed, blood sample analysis is currently the most accurate method of detecting recent drug use. Officials in two of the states that we selected said that it can be time consuming to obtain a search warrant for a blood sample, because it requires approval by a judge. For example, officials from a state highway-safety office stated that a DUID arrest can take 3 to 4 hours if blood is being collected, because arresting officers must wait for a warrant signed by a judge to conduct the blood test. Moreover, depending on local requirements and resources, potential offenders may need to be transported by law enforcement to a hospital or other location for a phlebotomist or nurse to collect a blood sample, leading to further delays.[30] As the arresting officer waits to collect the sample, the drug content in the suspect's blood can decrease significantly, resulting in a less accurate measure of the drug content in the blood at the time of the actual traffic stop.

Lab Backlogs Can Lead to Difficulties in Enforcement and Prosecution

According to toxicologists in four states, the lack of qualified lab personnel and testing equipment can contribute to a backlog of samples that need to be tested for drugs, which can result in long waits for toxicology results. In five of the states that we selected, officials told us that current lab backlogs ranged from no backlog to about 2,000 cases (the oldest case being 2 years old). As a result of a lab backlog, officials in two of the states that we selected said that a prosecutor may have to move forward with a drug-impaired driving case without toxicology results due to legal time constraints for prosecution. Additionally, toxicologists from two states said that some drug compounds continue to degrade once blood samples have been collected and may not be detectable in the sample three to six months after collection, making the evidence less useful or of no use to prosecutors.

Public Awareness about Dangers of Drugged Driving Is Limited

State prosecutors, toxicologists, law enforcement and highway-safety office officials from all of the selected states, as well as NIDA, told us that they believe that there is a lack of public awareness about the dangers of driving after using prescription medications and marijuana. According to prosecutors whom we spoke to in three states, alcohol-impaired driving is easy for people to understand, because the public has been educated about the dangers of drunk driving through various campaigns. However, they noted that people believe there is less danger associated with prescription medications and, in some cases, marijuana.

As a result, jurors may have a more difficult time understanding the dangers associated with driving under the influence of prescription medication, for example, based on their personal experience of taking similar medications without perceiving they are impaired or having a driving incident.

Additionally, according to state prosecutors, toxicologists and law-enforcement and highway-safety office officials from all of the selected states as well as NIDA, the public perceives that driving after using marijuana is not dangerous. Moreover, officials from two state highway safety offices and NIDA stated that in their view, the public is generally unaware of the unpredictable effects of combining multiple drugs. As a result of this perceived lack of awareness, members of the public may risk unknowingly driving while impaired, potentially leading to vehicle collisions, injuries, and fatalities.

Officials in four states said that there is a lack of focus on drug impairment in highway-safety public-education campaigns. For example, the traffic-safety-marketing communications resources available on NHTSA's website for states, partner organizations, and highway safety professionals who are related to impaired driving are generally focused on reducing drunk driving: "Drive Sober or Get Pulled Over" and "Buzzed Driving is Drunk Driving."

See figure 1. Additionally, campaigns in the states we selected generally use language that may suggest a focus on impairment due to alcohol, rather than drugs, for example, "Drive Hammered, Get Nailed."

Figure 1. NHTSA's "Drive Sober or Get Pulled Over" and "Buzzed Driving is Drunk Driving" Campaigns.

Federal and State Agencies Are Working to Address Drug-Impaired Driving, but NHTSA's Efforts to Improve Public Awareness Have Been Limited

Federal and selected state agencies are taking actions to address drug-impaired driving, including the challenges previously cited. These actions include improvements in the areas of research and data, education of law enforcement and court personnel, evidence quality, legal remedies, and public awareness. Furthermore, NHTSA, ONDCP, and states have coordinated their efforts to address drug-impaired driving challenges. However, NHTSA's current public awareness initiatives do not clearly include drug-impaired driving and state officials we spoke with stated that NHTSA could do more to increase public awareness about the dangers of drugged driving.

Research and Data on Drug-Impaired Driving

Research on Drug Impairment: Federal agencies have completed and are conducting research to increase knowledge about the relationship between drugs, impairment, and crash risk. For example, NHTSA is currently researching the crash risk of drug and alcohol use (including illegal, prescription, and OTC drugs) by collecting samples from more than 10,000 crash- and non crash-involved drivers in one city for 20 months. The results of this study are expected in 2015. Additionally, components of HHS, including NIDA, have researched the impairing effects of various drugs, including the effects of habitual marijuana use. For example, NIDA has conducted research on the length of time marijuana can be detected in blood after use (up to about 30 days in daily users). Regarding prescription and OTC drugs, the FDA uses information from studies conducted by drug manufacturers to assess new medications for adverse effects, including drowsiness, and requires that those effects are appropriately discussed in labeling, including package inserts.[31]

Data Availability, Consistency, and Timeliness: To increase the availability of data on drug-impaired driving, NHTSA has recommended that states distinguish among alcohol or drugs, or both for impaired driving cases. Some states, including Colorado and Arizona, are implementing systems to track whether impaired-driving arrests involved drugs or alcohol, or both. NHTSA officials stated that such state efforts may also help improve federal data sources, such as FARS. Additionally, California, Hawaii, and New York have separated driving under the influence of alcohol, drugs, or the combined influence of drugs and alcohol in their impaired driving statutes, a move that may result in more detailed data on the extent of drug-impaired and alcohol-impaired driving.

In 2013, the National Safety Council's Alcohol, Drugs and Impairment Division reviewed and updated a set of minimum recommendations to toxicologists for drug testing in suspected impaired-driving cases and fatal crashes, including recommendations to improve the consistency of data on the frequency with which specific drugs are linked with impaired driving.[32] Specifically, the recommendations included standards for the type of sample tested (blood, oral fluid, or urine), the scope of drugs for which to test, and cutoff values for reporting the presence of a drug. The NTSB has recommended that NHTSA develop and disseminate similar standards to state officials. According to NHTSA officials, they have discussed these types of standards with officials from SAMHSA, NTSB, and ONDCP. SAMHSA has recently developed oral fluid drug-testing standards for federal workplaces. These standards are currently under review and have not yet been released for public comment. NHTSA officials stated that they plan to wait until these workplace standards are further along in the approval process in order to develop guidance for states that are generally consistent with SAMHSA's workplace standards.

Further, some states have initiated or implemented plans to increase the capability of toxicology labs to improve the timeliness and availability of data. For example, Kansas has made recent efforts to increase the capacity of its forensic lab, housed in the Kansas Bureau of Investigation, through increased funding to retain specialized technicians, increased toxicology staffing, and building a new facility. According to an official from the lab, the improvements should help the state decrease its backlog of 2,000 toxicology cases (as of August 2014). Additionally, according to a lab official, the Ohio Crime Lab received federal grant funding in 2013 to purchase needed instrumentation and coordinates with the Indiana Department of Toxicology and the Kentucky State Police Toxicology Laboratories to share information and validation techniques for new drug- testing methodologies.

Education for Law Enforcement Officers and Legal Professionals

Drug Recognition Expert Program: One strategy for increasing knowledge about drug impairment among law enforcement mentioned by officials in all seven selected states is the Drug Recognition Expert (DRE) program, which provides training to law enforcement officers and others to identify drivers under the influence of drugs. For this program, IACP and NHTSA coordinated to leverage training originally developed in California.[33] The training includes 72 hours of classroom training and between 40 and 60 hours of field training. Law enforcement officers who complete this training are certified by states as Drug Recognition Experts (DRE) and qualified to perform a 12-step evaluation protocol to assess subjects for drug impairment, which includes psychophysical tests and physical examinations.

According to IACP's 2013 annual report on the DRE program, as of December 2013, about 6,750 DREs have been certified in all 50 states and the District of Columbia. [34] While officials in all of the selected states said that the DRE program was effective, some also discussed challenges related to the program, including:

- Training is time-consuming and expensive: Beyond the cost for training, which is often covered through state and federal grants, departments may need to pay for travel and lodging costs as well as overtime pay and additional coverage while officers attend training.
- Retention of certified officers: Officials from three selected states as well as IACP told us that high attrition among DREs makes it difficult to maintain enough certified officers. Reasons cited for this attrition include:

    - DRE-certified officers tend to be high-performing officers and are quickly promoted out of traffic units.
    - DRE re-certification requirements are time-consuming and expensive and may be difficult for small departments to fulfill.
- NHTSA's database of DRE reports is difficult to use: NHTSA maintains a database of DRE reports (submitted voluntarily by DRE officers) as a source of data on the program and drug-impaired driving. However, according to law enforcement officials from four of seven selected states, the DRE database is difficult to use, and the data are not currently available in a format that allows tracking of evaluations conducted by individual officers or departments. For example, officers from two states said that they have trouble accessing the system. They noted that, as such, some officers do not report evaluations, making the database incomplete. According to NHTSA officials, they periodically provide system improvements to make the database easier and more effective for officers to use; for example, they are currently determining what identifying information may be added to the system to make tracking easier, without compromising privacy or security. Additionally, NHTSA has plans to improve the system interface and software.

We were not able to identify any comprehensive study on the effectiveness of the program through our literature review, but NHTSA is currently conducting a study of a sample of DRE reports to examine the predictive validity of each of the components of the DRE evaluation; the results are expected in early 2015.

Advanced Roadside Impaired Driving Enforcement Program: In addition to the DRE program, law enforcement agencies in all seven of the states we selected have implemented Advanced Roadside Impaired Driving Enforcement (ARIDE) training, which is meant to bridge the gap between the basic training on impaired driving provided in most police academies and the more intensive DRE program. The 16-hour ARIDE training program, developed through coordination between NHTSA, IACP, and the Virginia Association of Chiefs of Police, trains officers to identify and assess drivers suspected of being under the influence of drugs. Additionally, ONDCP, NHTSA, and IACP have coordinated to create an online version of the ARIDE class, which could improve access to drug impairment evaluation training to law enforcement agencies with more limited resources. However, officials from five of the seven states said that they do not allow their officers to take the online version of the ARIDE class because, in their view, it is not a good substitute for the classroom training. NHTSA is currently conducting an evaluation of the ARIDE program, including a comparison of the original training with the online version, with an expected reporting date of early 2016.

Education for legal professionals: To increase the chances of successful prosecution of drug-impaired drivers, NHTSA grant funding may be used for state and regional level Traffic Safety Resource Prosecutor (TSRP) and Judicial Outreach Liaison (JOL) positions to provide training, education, and technical assistance to state prosecutors, judges, law enforcement officials, and toxicologists. For example, TSRPs in Arizona and California train toxicologists on providing effective testimony during trials. TSRPs also provide technical support to state and local prosecutors both generally and on a case-by-case basis to increase local ability to convict impaired drivers.

Guidance: Federal Agencies including NHTSA and DOJ have provided states with guidance regarding the enforcement of drug-impaired driving laws. For instance, DOJ's Community Oriented Policing Services component issued guidance on drug-impaired driving as part of its Problem-Specific Guides series. The guide includes a general description of drug-impaired driving and its causes as well as strategies to address enforcement challenges (many described above) and considerations for implementing the strategies described. Similarly, NHTSA published Saturation Patrols and Sobriety Checkpoints Guide: A How-to Guide for Planning and Publicizing Impaired Driving Enforcement Efforts, which guides state and local law enforcement agencies in planning and conducting high visibility enforcement campaigns (discussed below).

Actions to Preserve Evidence Quality

To improve the likelihood that drug testing results will accurately reflect drug concentrations at the time of a traffic stop or crash, some states have taken actions to reduce the time between initial contact with law enforcement and collection of evidence.

- **Roadside testing:** Development of an accurate roadside drug-testing device, comparable to breath sensors for alcohol detection could increase law enforcement officers' ability to identify drivers who have used drugs. Oral-fluid testing devices that are currently available test for a limited scope of drugs; representatives from SOFT stated that the scope includes the most common drugs found in drivers. NIH has conducted studies to validate the results of oral fluid and breath testing devices for certain drugs in controlled settings. Further, NHTSA is currently conducting research on the feasibility of incorporating available roadside oral fluid-testing devices in criminal justice processes, with results expected by early 2016. Additionally, a pilot program using various roadside oral fluid-testing devices has been conducted in Miami, with varying results depending on the device and type of drug. For example, one device was more accurate than the other overall, and accuracy for certain drugs was higher than for others.

- **Electronic warrant systems:** Washington and Arizona have established or are in the process of establishing electronic warrant systems, through which applications for warrants to collect biological samples are submitted, reviewed, and either granted or denied via electronic means (telephone, fax, or e-mail). According to law enforcement officials in those states, these systems can decrease the time between arrest and collection of samples for drug testing, in an effort to preserve evidence quality
- **Increased access to phlebotomy services:** For the past 8 to 9 years, Arizona has been training law enforcement officers as phlebotomists to reduce the time between arrest and collection of samples for drug testing, thus preserving evidence quality.

Legal Remedies

Sentencing policies: Officials from state agencies in four of seven states said that sentencing strategies such as the use of impaired-driving courts reduce recidivism through programs that use a model of post-conviction supervision and treatment, combined with punishment such as fines, in order to change behavior. We have previously reported that participants that received such additional supervision and treatment through adult drug courts, including designated impaired driving courts, were generally less likely to be re-arrested than comparison group members drawn from the criminal court system.[35]

Zero-tolerance per se laws: ONDCP, GHSA, and others have recommended that states establish "zero tolerance" laws, which make it illegal per se (in itself) to drive with a detectable amount of a prohibited drug (defined by state law) in one's system, regardless of whether there is evidence of impairment. According to a 2010 NHTSA report on the effectiveness of such laws, the compelling argument for zero tolerance laws is that, in their absence, a driver under the influence of an illegal substance was less likely to be prosecuted for impaired driving than a driver under the influence of alcohol. This problem existed because a maximum threshold linked to impairment has been established for alcohol, but there is no practical way to establish such a level for drugs. This study found some anecdotal support that zero tolerance laws increased prosecution rates, but a lack of reliable data prevented NHTSA from conclusively determining the effectiveness of such laws. Further, officials from NTSB stated there is no evidence that zero tolerance laws reduce impaired driving (since a driver need not be impaired to be prosecuted under the law). As of December 2014, 15 states have enacted laws that prohibit driving with a detectable prohibited substance in the driver's body, without any other evidence of impairment. For example, Illinois prohibits drivers from having a detectable amount of any illegal substance or other prohibited substances listed in the statute in his or her system, which would include certain medications such as hyoscyamine, which is used to control symptoms associated with gastrointestinal disorders. See figure 2.

Per se laws/drug concentration limits: Some officials recommend establishing "per se" limits, or thresholds, for certain drugs, similar to the 0.08 BAC limit established for alcohol. These laws make it illegal per se (in itself) for a driver to have a specific amount of a certain drug in his/her blood, oral fluid, or urine regardless of detectable impairment. As of December 2014, six states have enacted per se laws based on drug concentration limits for one or more drugs (see fig. 2). For instance, Washington has established a limit of 5 nanograms of THC per milliliter of blood for drivers.[36] Colorado has implemented a similar law establishing 5 nanograms of THC per milliliter of blood as a "permissible inference," which, according to a state official, means jurors may infer that the defendant was impaired but are not required to do so.[37]

Additionally, Nevada and Ohio have developed per se thresholds for certain controlled substances including illegal drugs such as cocaine and heroin as well as legal drugs such as amphetamines, which can be used to treat conditions such as attention deficit disorder and narcolepsy.[38]

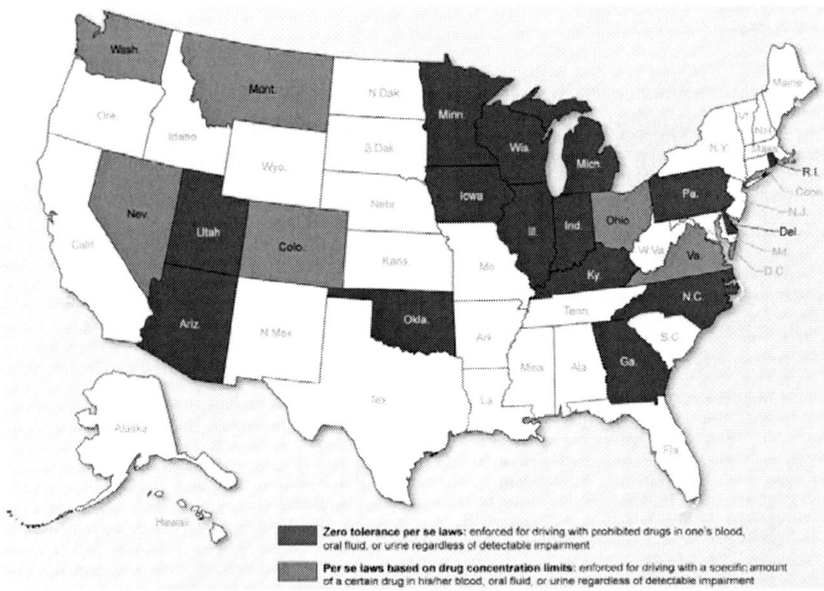

Notes: This map does not include state laws specifically applicable to individuals under 21. This map is based on GAO analysis of state laws as of December 3, 2014.

Figure 2. Map of States with Zero-Tolerance Per Se Laws and Per Se Laws Based on Drug Concentration Limits, as of December 2014.

Per se laws based on drug concentration limits may increase prosecutions for drivers who are over the established limits, but the effectiveness of these laws is unknown and may have unintended consequences. Officials from Colorado, Ohio, and SOFT stated that per se limits make prosecution of drivers who are over the limits more likely. However, others, including officials from California and Washington, stated that it may also make prosecution of drivers who were observed to be impaired but whose drug test results were under the established limit more difficult: once thresholds are established, drivers and jurors may develop the false assumption that driving below the established limit is legal, even if there is observable impairment. Some toxicologists, including representatives from SOFT, stated that per se laws based on thresholds may serve a particular policy goal of increasing prosecutions, but that a link between the established thresholds and impairment levels cannot be supported scientifically. A representative from SOFT also stated that, because illegal drugs generally have no medical purpose, there is a significant difference between establishing per se threshold levels for illegal drugs versus per se threshold levels for prescription and OTC medications. According to the representative, setting per se limits for prescription and OTC medications may cause problems for those who are taking medications as prescribed and may not be impaired.

Efforts to Increase Public Awareness about DUID

Some federal and selected state agencies have implemented drug-impaired driving awareness campaigns to increase public knowledge about the dangers of drugged driving. For instance, ONDCP developed the *Teen Drugged Driving: Parent, Coalition, and Community Group Activity Guide*, which provides coalitions, prevention groups, and parent organizations with facts on the dangers and extent of teen and young adult drugged driving, parent and community activities for effective prevention, and resources to further assist in prevention activities. At the state level, Colorado, Washington, and Ohio have conducted public awareness campaigns focused on drug-impaired driving. For example, Colorado has aired a series of public service announcements focusing on the dangers of driving after using marijuana and emphasizing that driving impaired remains illegal, even as marijuana has been legalized at the state level.

While NHTSA has also established impaired-driving public awareness programs, materials associated with these programs do not explicitly include information on the dangers of drug-impaired driving. NHTSA's public awareness programs include high-visibility enforcement campaigns such as the "Drive Sober or Get Pulled Over" and "Buzzed Driving is Drunk Driving" campaigns (see fig. 1, presented previously), which according to NHTSA officials, include drug-impaired driving. For these campaigns, NHTSA provides media, such as television and radio advertisements, to states to help inform the public about the dangers of impaired driving and provides grant funding for state and local police to perform highly visible checkpoints and patrols to reinforce the concept that impaired drivers are at a high risk of being caught and prosecuted. However, using the terms "sober" and "drunk" in the campaign slogans may indicate that the campaigns are about the dangers of driving after consuming alcohol as opposed to drugs.

NHTSA's mission is to support state traffic safety efforts. However, officials from six of seven selected states as well as representatives from GHSA stated that public education more explicitly focused on the dangers of drugged driving is needed, particularly on impairment due to prescription and

OTC medications and marijuana. Officials from some states recommended actions such as increased education and requirements for medical professionals regarding prescription drug use and drug-impaired driving, but also recommended that NHTSA expand the current messaging on impairment to include the dangers of marijuana and prescription drugs, which are not explicitly addressed through NHTSA's impaired driving advertising campaigns.

According to NHTSA officials, the current lack of data on impairment thresholds and the broad range of drug effects make it more difficult to concisely communicate the dangers of drug-impaired driving compared to alcohol-impaired driving and has prevented them from including drugs more explicitly in current messaging. However, the messaging for current alcohol-impaired driving campaigns—such as Drive Sober or Get Pulled Over—does not specifically allude to the .08 BAC limit. Increased focus on information about the potential dangers of driving after using drugs could provide an important reminder to drivers that alcohol is not the only substance that may impair driving ability. Adding more explicit messaging about drug-impaired driving could be relatively simple, and could potentially reduce crashes and associated injuries and fatalities.

NHTSA officials also said they have other plans to improve public awareness about the dangers of drug-impaired driving. For example, NHTSA officials plan to conduct a recurring survey of driver attitudes and behaviors regarding drugged and drug-impaired driving. Data from this survey could help NHTSA more fully understand any gaps in public awareness about the dangers of drug-impaired driving and develop appropriate public awareness campaigns to address those gaps. NHTSA officials also plan to provide training for physicians and other medical professionals on how to inform patients about the dangers of driving after taking some prescription and OTC medications. These efforts to improve public awareness are in the initial planning stages and could take several years to implement.

Coordination among Federal and State Agencies

To leverage the expertise of various stakeholders to address drug-impaired driving, federal agencies—including NHTSA, ONDCP, HHS, NTSB, and states—have coordinated to identify strategies to address drug-impaired driving. For instance, ONDCP and NHTSA convened a roundtable of drug testing and criminal justice experts to examine new drug testing technology in

2012, and have since coordinated to initiate the additional research and testing of roadside oral-fluid-testing devices previously discussed. Additionally, Colorado and Washington have established impaired-driving working groups to develop and implement strategies for addressing drug- and alcohol-impaired driving. These working groups include state and local law-enforcement, traffic-safety, public-health, and motor-vehicle agencies as well as representatives from the court system, professional organizations, the marijuana industry, and others.

CONCLUSION

The lack of complete and reliable data on the extent and nature of drug-impaired driving presents federal, state, and local agencies with challenges to developing and implementing effective countermeasures. Ongoing and planned activities by NHTSA, ONDCP, and others are intended to increase available information on drug-impaired driving and strategies to address the problem, and coordination across the various federal, state, and local stakeholders is essential to fully implement any strategy. For example, development and validation of a roadside oralfluid-testing device may improve evidence collection processes for local and state law enforcement, but continued efforts to standardize lab procedures, collect and maintain data, educate law enforcement to recognize potential drug impairment, and educate prosecutors are also important to realize the benefits of faster evidence collection.

Despite limited data and the challenge of defining impairment, federal and state agencies have identified and implemented promising activities— such as the DRE Program, initiatives to reduce the time to collect and analyze evidence, and public awareness—to combat drug-impaired driving and associated crashes, fatalities, and injuries. For example, the DRE Program and high-visibility enforcement campaigns have already been implemented in many jurisdictions. NHTSA and other federal agencies have initiated, supported, and continue to improve these activities. However, state officials consistently noted that their public awareness efforts would benefit from additional support from NHTSA to help increase public knowledge of the potential dangers of drug-impaired driving, including impairment due to some prescription medications and marijuana. While NHTSA's plans to improve public awareness of drug-impaired driving through a survey on public behaviors and attitudes and training for medical professionals are promising, these initiatives will take time to implement. Additional efforts, such as general messaging reminding the public about the impairing effects of some drugs and the dangers of driving after using drugs, could help improve public awareness in the near term.

Recommendation

We recommend that the Secretary of Transportation direct the Administrator of NHTSA to identify actions—in addition to the agency's currently planned efforts—to support state efforts to increase public awareness of the dangers of drug-impaired driving. This effort should be undertaken in consultation with ONDCP, HHS, state highway-safety offices, and other interested parties as needed.

Agency Comments

We provided a draft of this report to DOT, ONDCP, and HHS for review and comment. In written comments, DOT agreed with our findings and recommendation. ONDCP had no comments. HHS provided technical comments, which we incorporated as appropriate.

Susan A. Fleming
Director, Physical Infrastructure Issues

Appendix I: Objectives, Scope, and Methodology

The Senate Report accompanying the Transportation and Housing and Urban Development, and Related Agencies Appropriations Bill, 2014[1] requires us to conduct a study on the strategies that NHTSA, ONDCP, and states have taken to address drug impairment and assess the challenges they face in detecting and reducing drug-impaired driving. Pursuant to that mandate, we reviewed the actions of relevant federal agencies and selected states as well as relevant literature to identify actions taken to address drug-impaired driving and associated challenges. Specifically, we analyzed (1) what is known about the extent of drug-impaired driving in the United States; (2) what challenges, if any, exist for federal, state, and local agencies in addressing drug-impaired driving; and (3) what actions federal and state agencies have taken to address drug-impaired driving and what gaps exist, if any, in the federal response to drug-impaired driving. This review defines drug-impaired driving as driving while impaired by illegal drugs or prescription and over-the-counter (legal) medications. This review does not include impaired driving among commercial motor carriers, for which different laws and regulations apply than for members of the general public.

To describe what is known about the extent of drug-impaired driving in the United States, to identify challenges to addressing drug-impaired driving, and to identify actions federal and state agencies have taken to mitigate those challenges, we conducted a literature search to identify sources of data on the extent of drugged and drug-impaired driving in the United States and studies on the issue of drug-impaired driving, including challenges and strategies for addressing the problem. We identified existing studies from peer-reviewed journals, government reports, and conference papers based on searches of various databases, such as ProQuest and Transportation Research International Documentation. Search parameters included international studies, studies across the U.S. and in specific states, and research on drug-impaired-driving challenges and countermeasures. These parameters resulted in 394 abstracts, which we narrowed to 225 by eliminating, for example, studies addressing only the extent of drugged or drug-impaired driving in countries other than the United States or studies on the broader topic of drug abuse. We further divided the literature into studies on the extent of drugged or drug-impaired driving in the United States and studies on drug-impaired driving challenges and countermeasures. Studies including data on the extent of drugged or drug-impaired driving in the United States were reviewed to identify the source of the data and limitations. We reviewed these studies and determined that they were sufficiently reliable for the purposes of this report. Studies on countermeasures to address drug-impaired driving and challenges were used to provide additional context and information when needed. We also reviewed state laws to develop information regarding state zero-tolerance per se laws and state per se laws based on drug concentration limits.

Additionally, we reviewed documentation, such as research studies and plans and agency guidance, and interviewed officials from relevant governmental and non-governmental organizations to identify (1) sources of data and their limitations, (2) challenges to addressing drug-impaired driving, and (3) actions taken by federal and state agencies to address drug-impaired driving as well as gaps in the federal response. Federal agencies, advocacy organizations, and professional organizations were chosen based on having a mission relevant to the issue of drug-impaired driving and recommendations from relevant stakeholders. We interviewed officials at relevant federal agencies including the National Highway Traffic Safety Administration (NHTSA); the White House's Office of National Drug Control Policy (ONDCP); National Transportation Safety Board (NTSB); and Department of Health and Human Services' (HHS) components including the Substance Abuse and Mental Health Services Administration (SAMHSA), Centers for Disease Control and Prevention (CDC), Food and Drug Administration (FDA), and National Institutes of Health (NIH).[2] Additionally, we reviewed documentation obtained from and interviewed officials in seven states: Arizona, California, Colorado, Kansas, Ohio, Vermont, and Washington. We reviewed documentation and interviewed officials at state agencies responsible for highway-safety and drug-impairment programs, advocacy organizations, and professional organizations based on recommendations from the state highway-safety office. For example, we interviewed officials from state highway-safety offices, departments of public health and motor vehicles, state law- enforcement agencies, Drug Recognition Expert (DRE) program coordinators, state Traffic Safety Resource Prosecutors (TSRP), associations of police chiefs and district attorneys, state and local toxicologists, and local interest groups. We selected these states based on recommendations from federal officials and representatives from advocacy and professional organizations and to represent a variety of laws, programs, and other factors. Our selection included:

- states with legalized recreational marijuana,
- states that geographically border states in which recreational marijuana use has been legalized,
- states with legalized medical marijuana,
- states representing a variety of drug-impaired driving laws, and
- states identified as having robust programs dealing with driving under the influence of drugs.

We also reviewed documentation and interviewed representatives from advocacy and professional organizations including the Governors Highway Safety Association (GHSA), National District Attorneys Association, Society of Forensic Toxicologists, Inc. (SOFT), Mothers Against Drunk Driving (MADD), International Association of Chiefs of Police (IACP), Insurance

Institute for Highway Safety, and National Council of State Legislatures (NCSL).

We conducted this performance audit from April 2014 through February 2015 in accordance with generally accepted government auditing standards. Those standards require that we plan and perform the audit to obtain sufficient, appropriate evidence to provide a reasonable basis for our findings and conclusions based on our audit objectives. We believe the evidence obtained provides a reasonable basis for our findings and conclusions based on our audit objectives.

End Notes

[1] A. Berning, R. Compton, and K. Wochinger, *Results of the 2013-2014 National Roadside Survey of alcohol and drug use by drivers* (Traffic Safety Facts Research Note. Report No. DOT HS 812 118, U.S. Dept. of Transportation, National Highway Traffic Safety Administration, Washington, D.C.: 2015). These results are an estimate of the prevalence of drivers with detectable amounts of drugs in their systems and do not imply impairment. The *National Roadside Survey* is a survey sponsored by the National Highway Traffic Safety Administration that indicates the extent to which people drive with drugs present in their system, and is representative of the United States. This survey was conducted in 2013-2014, with full results expected in 2015.

[2] For the purposes of this report, the term "drugged driving" refers to driving with any detectable amount of drugs in one's system, as opposed to "drug-impaired driving," which refers to driving while impaired to some degree from using drugs. ONDCP's goal is to reduce the prevalence of drugged driving by 10 percent as compared to a 2009 baseline, established by the Department of Health and Human Services' Substance Abuse and Mental Health Services Administration's 2009 National Survey on Drug Use and Health.

[3] S. Rep. No.113-45 (2013).

[4] Within NIH, the National Institute on Drug Abuse (NIDA) is the primary institute involved in this topic. NIDA is one of the 27 institutes and centers within the National Institutes of Health.

[5] Under MAP-21, 52.5 percent of the total amount of National Priority Safety Program funds are available for impaired-driving countermeasures, with up to 15 percent of those funds available for incentive grants for ignition interlocks—devices that prevent drivers from starting their cars if they have been drinking alcohol. Any of the remaining funding is available for other impaired-driving countermeasures, funding that is allocated to states for eligible impaired-driving activities, including countermeasures for alcohol- and drug-impaired driving. Pub. L. No. 112-141, § 31105(a), 126 Stat. 405, 748 (2012). MAP-21 expired September 30, 2014. Programs and budget authority authorized under MAP-21 were extended until May 31, 2015 by Pub. L. No. 113-159,128 Stat. 1839 (2014). The National Priority Safety Programs were authorized $181,084,932 for the period between October 1, 2014, and May 31, 2015.

[6] "Per se BAC laws" establish the BAC level at which it is illegal per se (in itself) for a driver to operate a vehicle, regardless of the driver's apparent condition or actions.

[7] Over-the-counter drugs are those that can be purchased without a doctor's prescription, including some pain-relievers, cold and cough medicines, and others.

[8] In November 2014, ballot initiatives legalizing recreational marijuana passed in Alaska, Oregon, and the District of Columbia; these initiatives have not taken effect as of the beginning of February 2015.

[9] Toxicology results are the result of laboratory testing of biological samples of bodily fluid for the presence of various substances.

[10] Lacey et al. The *NRS* methodology involves randomly stopping drivers at locations across the United States to conduct voluntary surveys and collect biological samples after obtaining consent. Drivers who participated were tested for illegal, prescription, and OTC drugs through analyses of oral fluid, blood, and breath specimens taken during key periods during which impaired driving most often occurs. Drugs tested were chosen in part due to their potential to impair driving performance.

[11] A. Berning, R. Compton, and K. Wochinger, *Results of the 2013-2014 National Roadside Survey*.

[12] Lacey, John H; Kelley-Baker, Tara, et. Al, *2012 California Roadside Survey of Nighttime Weekend Drivers' Alcohol and Drug Use* (Pacific Institute for Research and Evaluation, Calverton, MD: 2012).

[13] NRS respondents completed a paper-and-pencil, drug-use-disorder screening instrument. In the 2013 NRS, in addition to an oral fluid test, the driver was asked additional questions about prescription drug use. For the California survey, respondents were asked questions covering drug use.

[14] These findings may be in part due to the fact that some drugs, such as marijuana, remain detectable in human fluids for days or weeks after they have been ingested

[15] Substance Abuse and Mental Health Services Administration, *Results from the 2012 National Survey on Drug Use and Health: Summary of National Findings*, NSDUH Series H-46, HHS Publication No. (SMA) 13-4795 (Rockville, MD: 2013).

[16] From 2008 to 2012, the percentage of respondents reporting driving under the influence of drug varied from 3.7 to 4.2 percent, but due to sampling error the actual differences from year to year may be insignificant. Respondents to the survey are age 12 and older.

[17] NIDA's College Life Study is a longitudinal study of 1,253 college students at a large, public, mid-Atlantic university aimed at discovering the impact of health-related behaviors during the college experience.

[18] Bachman, J. G., Johnston, L. D., and O'Malley, P. M., *Monitoring the Future: Questionnaire responses from the nation's high school seniors, 2012* (Institute for Social Research, Ann Arbor, MI: 2014). The 2012 *Monitoring the Future* survey provides estimates for a nationally representative sample of high school seniors on an annual basis. The survey does not include in its target population those who drop out of high school before the last few months of their senior year, and so excludes a relatively small proportion of each age cohort, but may disproportionately exclude those who have a tendency toward certain behaviors such as illegal drug use. The overall student response rate for 2012 was reported to be 83 percent.

[19] The California vehicle code is now composed of separate reportable sections on DUI alcohol, DUI Drugs, and DUI Combination alcohol and drugs.

[20] Couper, Fiona; Peterson, Briana, "The Prevalence of Marijuana in Suspected Impaired Driving Cases in Washington State," *Journal of Analytical Toxicology*, 18-Mar (2014). Tetrahydrocannabinol (THC) is the main psychoactive compound found in the cannabis (marijuana) plant.

[21] For instance, under the Drug Free Workplace Program (established in accordance with Exec. Order No. 12564, 51 Fed. Reg. 32889 (Sept. 15,1986) a supplemental appropriations act for fiscal year 1987, Pub. L. No. 100 -71, 191 Stat. 468 (1987) and the *Mandatory Guidelines for Federal Workplace Drug Testing Programs*, 73 Fed. Reg. 71858 (Nov. 25, 2008)), the SAMHSA National Laboratory Certification Program establishes standards for federal workplace drug testing. The National Commission on Forensic Science, a partnership between the Department of Justice and the Department of Commerce's National Institute of Standards and Technology, is currently working to develop guidance regarding universal accreditation for forensic-science service providers.

[22] Laurel J. Farrell, Sarah Kerrigan, and Barry K. Logan, "Recommendations for Toxicological Investigation of Drug Impaired Driving," *Journal of Forensic Sciences, vol. 52 no. 5 (2007).*

[23] FARS is a nationwide census providing NHTSA, Congress, and the American public yearly data regarding fatal injuries suffered in motor vehicle traffic crashes.

[24] Blood and breath tests are two different methods for measuring an individual's blood alcohol level.

[25] FDA, *Some Medications and Driving Don't Mix*, updated October 14, 2014. http://www.fda.gov/ForConsumers/ConsumerUpdates/ucm107894.htm.

[26] B.K. Logan, K. J Lowrie, J. L. Turri, J. K. Yeakel, J. F. Limoges, A. K. Miles, C. E. Scarneo, S. Kerrigan, and L. J. Farrell, "Recommendations for Toxicological Investigation of Drug-Impaired Driving and Motor Vehicle Fatalities," Journal of Analytical Toxicology, vol. 37 (2013).

[27] Synthetic drugs are chemically produced in a laboratory and may be developed to circumvent current drug laws and testing. The chemical structure for synthetics can be either identical to or different from naturally occurring drugs, and their effects may be designed to mimic or even increase the effects of natural drugs.

[28] United Nations Office on Drugs and Crime. *World Drug Report 2013* (May 2013).

[29] While some oral fluid and breath testing devices have been developed to detect drug use, they have not yet been validated for use in the field.

[30] A phlebotomist is an individual trained to draw blood for tests, transfusions, research, or blood donations.

[31] According to HHS, although the carton or container of a prescription drug supplied by the manufacturer may include information concerning adverse effects, such as drowsiness, state boards of pharmacies regulate the label of the repackaged container that is dispensed to patients.

[32] The National Safety Council is a nonprofit advocacy organization focused on preventing injuries and fatalities through research, education, and advocacy. B.K. Logan, K. J Lowrie, J. L. Turri, J. K. Yeakel, J. F. Limoges, A. K. Miles, C. E. Scarneo, S. Kerrigan, and L. J. Farrell, "Recommendations for Toxicological Investigation of Drug-Impaired Driving and Motor Vehicle Fatalities," *Journal of Analytical Toxicology*, vol. 37, no. 8 (2013).

[33] DREs are trained through the Drug Evaluation and Classification Program, coordinated by the IACP with support from NHTSA.

[34] International Association of Chiefs of Police, *The 2013 Annual Report of the IACP Drug Recognition Section* (Alexandria, VA: Oct. 20, 2014).

[35] GAO, *Adult Drug Courts: Studies Show Courts Reduce Recidivism, but DOJ Could Enhance Future Performance Measure Revision Efforts*, GAO-12-53 (Washington, D.C.: Dec. 9, 2011).

[36] Wash. Rev. Code Ann. § 46.61.502(1)(a)-(b). A nanogram is equal to one billionth of one gram.
[37] Colo. Rev. Stat. Ann. § 42-4-1301(1)(a)-(c).
[38] Nev. Rev. Stat. Ann. § 484C.120, Ohio Rev. Code § 4511.19.

End Notes for Appendix I

[1] S. Rep. No. 113-45 (2013).
[2] Within NIH, the National Institute on Drug Abuse (NIDA) is the primary institute involved in this topic. NIDA is one of the 27 institutes and centers within the National Institutes of Health.

In: Drug-Impaired Driving
Editor: Tobias H. Erickson

ISBN: 978-1-63482-871-0

Chapter 2

DRUG AND ALCOHOL CRASH RISK*

Richard P. Compton and Amy Berning

BACKGROUND AND INTRODUCTION

While the extent of use of alcohol by drivers and the risks posed by alcohol use have been well known for many decades, relatively little has been known about the use of other drugs by drivers and the associated risks. However, drug-impaired driving has recently become an issue of increasing public and governmental concern in the United States and in many other countries (Compton et al., 2009; Asbridge et al., 2012; ICADTS, 2007). While it is readily apparent that driving-related skills can be impaired by a wide variety of illegal substances and medications, the nature and scope of the drug-impaired driving problem has been difficult to define (Jones et al., 2003; DuPont et al., 2012; Houwing, 2013). In the United States, recent State actions to legalize the use of marijuana for medical and recreational use have further exacerbated concern over potential risks of driving impaired by marijuana.

Marijuana is the most frequently detected drug (other than alcohol) in crash-involved drivers as well as the general driving population (Terhune, 1982; Terhune et al., 1992; Lacey et al., 2009; Walsh et al., 2005). There is evidence that marijuana use impairs psychomotor skills, divided attention, lane

---

* This is an edited, reformatted and augmented version of a Traffic Safety Facts Research Note, Report No. DOT HS 812 117, issued by the National Highway Traffic Safety Administration, Office of Behavioral Safety Research, February 2015.

tracking, and cognitive functions (Robbe et al., 1993; Moskowitz, 1995; Hartman and Huestis, 2013). However, its role in contributing to the occurrence of crashes remains less clear. Many studies, using a variety of methods have attempted to estimate the risk of driving after use of marijuana (Li et al., 2012; Asbridge et al., 2012). The methods have included experimental studies, observational studies, and epidemiological studies. While useful in identifying how marijuana affects the performance of driving tasks, experimental and observational studies do not lend themselves to predicting real world crash risk.

EPIDEMIOLOGICAL STUDIES

Epidemiological studies differ in how they estimate risk. Culpability studies compare the rate at which crash-involved, drug-positive drivers and drug-negative drivers are deemed to be at fault for their crashes. Case-control studies compare drug use by crash-involved drivers to drug use by non-crash involved drivers. In general, the case-control method is preferable since it can eliminate more sources of potential bias in estimating crash risk resulting from drug use (e.g., alcohol use is much higher at night and on weekends than during the day or on weekdays). The existing epidemiological research (both culpability and case-control studies) have produced contradictory estimates of risk for marijuana use. Some of these studies have suggested that marijuana use has minimal or no effect on the likelihood of crash involvement, while others have estimated a small increase in the risk of crash involvement.

Two recent population-based case control studies have estimated the crash risk of drug use by drivers by using NHTSA's Fatality Analysis Reporting System (FARS) 2007 data for the crash-involved driver population and the 2007 National Roadside Survey of Alcohol and Drug Use by Drivers for the control drivers (Lia, Bradya, & Chen, 2013; Romano, Torres-Saavedra, Voas, & Lacey, 2014). The Li study estimated the increased risk of crash involvement for drivers using marijuana at 1.83 times that of drug-free drivers, while the Romano study found no increased risk of crash involvement for those drivers testing positive for THC (the main psychoactive substance in marijuana). However, current limitations in the FARS dataset do not allow calculation of unbiased, reliable and valid estimates of the risk of crash involvement that results from drug use.

CHALLENGES IN ESTIMATING CRASH RISK FROM DRUG USE

Conducting case-control studies to estimate the risk of crash involvement from drug use presents many difficulties. The first challenge has been getting reliable and accurate estimates of drug use. Many studies rely on self-report (which have obvious inherent problems) rather than actual measurement of THC in blood or oral fluid.

Also, the method of selecting truly comparable control drivers in an unbiased fashion for the crash involved drivers has varied considerably. The more carefully controlled studies, that actually measured marijuana (THC) use by drivers rather than relying on self-report, and that had more actual control of covariates that could bias the results, generally show reduced risk estimates or no risk associated with marijuana use (Elvik, 2013).

META-ANALYSIS

For example, a recent meta-analysis by Li (2012) used nine studies, five of which were based on self-report; of the remaining four studies, marijuana use was inferred from a urine test in three of the studies (which really only indicates the drivers were marijuana users but not necessarily had used marijuana prior to driving). The studies that used self-reporting produced increased crash risk estimates that ranged from 1.7 to 7.16 times as a result of marijuana use by drivers. The two studies that used urine to determine marijuana use resulted in risk estimates of 0.85 to 3.43 times, while the two studies using blood analysis had risk estimates of 2.10 and 2.11 times. The overall pooled risk estimate was 2.66 times.

Similarly, a meta-analysis by Asbridge (2012) also used nine studies, but six were culpability studies with only three using a case-control approach. One of the culpability studies used only FARS data and was of questionable value. Of the three using case-control methods, two used self-report by the control drivers and one used non-drug positive crash-involved drivers (meaning the controls were drug-free, crash-involved drivers). The risk estimates resulting from marijuana use ranged from 0.82 to 7.16 (two studies showing marijuana use reduced the risk of crash involvement while seven studies showed an increased risk). The pooled odds ratio for all nine studies was 1.92.

Recently, a fairly large-scale population-based case control study (in which an attempt was made to have the crash and non-crash control drivers represent all crash-involved drivers and all non-crash involved drivers in the same jurisdiction) was conducted by the European Union to estimate the crash risk of drug use by drivers. A population-based study can benefit from a large sample of drivers covering a wide geographic area which may improve the generalizability of findings. However, the scale of such studies typically limits the control of subject selection. In a population-based case control study, the case and control drivers are selected from different sources. For example, the crash-involved drivers might be injured drivers taken to a hospital after a crash, while the control drivers might be selected from general traffic. This method lacks the careful matching (day of week, time of day, location, direction of travel, etc.) used in smaller-scale studies, so it involves some compromise of control for the benefit of a much larger sample size.

DRUID Study

The recent population-based study known as Driving Under the Influence of Drugs, Alcohol and Medicines (DRUID), is the largest study of this type (Hels et al., 2010). This study, conducted in nine European Union (EU) countries: Belgium, Denmark, Finland, Italy, Lithuania, and the Netherlands used seriously injured crash-involved drivers while Norway, Portugal, and Sweden used fatally injured drivers. The crash-involved fatally injured driver sample came from a group of drivers for whom a drug test had been conducted, over a period of two to three years. Seriously injured drivers came from a sample of drivers taken to a hospital. Controls came from a roadside survey conducted in each of the respective countries, around the same general time period (e.g., over a year) in each country and represented a sample of drivers, in some cases, from the same general area from which the fatally and seriously injured drivers' crashes occurred. However, in only two of the countries did the controls come from the exact same area of the country as the crash-involved drivers. The specific locations of the crashes were not matched to the sites used to obtain the non-crash involved control drivers. Also, drug presence was determined from blood samples for all the crash-involved drivers, but eight of the countries used oral fluid to determine drug presence in the non-crash involved drivers (four countries also used blood for some control drivers).

Odds ratios were used to estimate the risk of crash involvement after marijuana use in the fatally and seriously injured drivers. The results for the seriously injured drivers showed considerable national variability, ranging from 0.29 times (reduced crash involvement) to 25.38 times (increased crash involvement). The combined risk was 1.39 times that of drug-free drivers, but this was not statistically significant. For fatally injured drivers the estimated risk ranged from 3.91 to 28.88, while the combined risk was 1.33 times (also not statistically significant).

In a pooled analysis of the DRUID data, the highest risk of crash involvement was for drivers with high alcohol concentrations (above .12 BAC)—they had a crash risk 20–200 times that of sober drivers. Drivers with BACs between .08 and .12 were estimated to be 5–30 times more likely to crash than sober drivers. Drivers positive for THC were estimated to be at elevated risk (1–3 times that of sober drivers), similar to drivers with BAC levels between .01 to < 0.05. The DRUID report noted that some of the risk estimates were based on few positive cases and/or controls which resulted in wide confidence intervals.

In order to further understand the risk of drug use by drivers, the National Highway Traffic Safety Administration (NHTSA), with funding support from the National Institute on Alcohol Abuse and Alcoholism (NIAAA), contracted with the Pacific Institute for Research and Evaluation (PIRE) to conduct the largest and most comprehensive study to address alcohol and drug crash risk in the United States through a case-control study, that employed a rigorous design involving a precise matching of cases and controls.

This case control study collected information from crash-involved and non-crash involved drivers for 20 months in Virginia Beach, Virginia.

NHTSA's "Crash Risk" Study

The case control crash risk study reported here is the first large-scale study in the United States to include drugs other than alcohol. It was designed to estimate the risk associated with alcohol- and drug-positive driving. Virginia Beach, Virginia, was selected for this study because of the outstanding cooperation of the Virginia Beach Police Department and other local agencies with our stringent research protocol. Another reason for selection was that Virginia Beach is large enough to provide a sufficient number of crashes for meaningful analysis. Data was collected from more than 3,000 crash-involved drivers and 6,000 control drivers (not involved in crashes). Breath alcohol measurements were obtained from a total of 10,221 drivers, oral fluid samples from 9,285 drivers, and blood samples from 1,764 drivers.

Research teams responded to crashes 24 hours a day, 7 days a week over a 20-month period. In order to maximize comparability, efforts were made to match control drivers to each crash-involved driver. One week after a driver involved in a crash provided data for the study, control drivers were selected at the same location, day of week, time of day, and direction of travel as the original crash. This allowed a comparison to be made between use of alcohol and other drugs by drivers involved in a crash with drivers not in a crash, resulting in an estimation of the relative risk of crash involvement associated with alcohol or drug use. In this study, the term marijuana is used to refer to drivers who tested positive for delta-9-tetrahydrocannabinal (THC). THC is associated with the psychoactive effects of ingesting marijuana. Drivers who tested positive for inactive cannabinoids were not considered positive for marijuana. More information on the methodology of this study and other methods of estimating crash risk is presented later in this Research Note.

DRUGS FOUND IN CRASH-INVOLVED AND CONTROL DRIVERS

Tables 1 and 2 show the number and percent of drivers that were positive for various classes and types of drugs. The use of alcohol is not included in these two tables. The drug most frequently used by drivers was THC, detected in 7.6 percent (n = 234) of the crash-involved drivers and 6.1 percent (n = 379) of the control drivers. In contrast, alcohol was detected in 5.0 percent (n = 168) of the crash-involved drivers and 2.7 percent (n = 187) of the control drivers (Table 7). The next most frequently detected drugs were narcotic-analgesics (opiates) found in 3.4 percent (n = 105) of the crash-involved drivers and 3.0 percent (n = 188) of the control drivers, followed by stimulants with 3.8 percent (n = 116) of the crash-involved drivers and 3.6 percent (n = 225) of the control drivers, with sedatives found in 2.9 percent (n = 90) of the crash-involved drivers and 2.3 percent (n = 139) of the control drivers.

Some 3.0 percent (n = 92) of the crash-involved drivers tested positive for more than one class of drug, while 2.1 percent (n = 132) of the control drivers tested positive for more than one drug. Based on simple proportions, crash-involved drivers were significantly more likely to test positive for THC and sedatives, to have used more than one class of drug, and to have used any type of drug than were control drivers. In this paper, p-values < 0.05 are considered statistically significant.

Table 1. Percent Crash and Control Drivers Positive by Drug Classes (Oral Fluid)

Drug or Drug Class	Crash		Control		P Value
	N	%	N	%	
THC (Marijuana)	234	7.6%	379	6.1%	0.01
Stimulants	116	3.8%	225	3.6%	0.78
Narcotic-Analgesics	105	3.4%	188	3.0%	0.36
Sedatives	90	2.9%	139	2.3%	0.05
Antidepressants	44	1.4%	82	1.3%	0.70
Other	23	0.7%	30	0.5%	0.12
More than 1 Class	92	3.0%	132	2.1%	0.01
Overall Drug Positive	495	16.0%	889	14.4%	0.04
Negative	2,600	84.0%	5,301	85.6%	0.04
All	3,095		6,190		

Some drivers were positive for more than one drug. Thus, the sum of the number of drugs detected will be larger than the number of drivers positive for drugs. P-Values based on z test of proportions (equivalent to Pearson's Chi Square). Shading indicates statistical significance (<0.05) between crash and control drivers.

Caution should be exercised in assuming that drug presence implies driver impairment. Drug tests do not necessarily indicate current impairment. Also, in some cases, drug presence can be detected for a period of days or weeks after ingestion.

Table 2. Percent Crash and Control Drivers Positive by Drug Type (Oral Fluid)

Drug Category	Crash		Control		P Value
	N	%	N	%	
Illegal	322	10.4%	546	8.8%	0.01
Legal	173	5.6%	343	5.5%	0.92
Negative	2,600	84.0%	5,301	85.6%	0.04
All	3,095	100.0%	6,190	100.0%	

P-Values based on z test of proportions (equivalent to Pearson's Chi Square). Shading indicates statistical significance.

Looking at the differences between illegal drugs and legal drugs (which may have been used according to a prescription or used illegally), there appears to be virtually no difference in the percentage of crash-involved drivers testing positive for legal drugs at 5.6 percent (n = 173) and control drivers testing positive for legal drugs at 5.5 percent (n = 343). However, that is not the case for illegal drugs, where statistically significantly more of the crash-involved drivers tested positive at 10.4 percent (n = 322), while 8.8 percent (n = 546) of control drivers tested positive for illegal drugs (see Table 2).

DRUG RELATIVE CRASH RISK ESTIMATES

To estimate the risk of crashing associated with drug use, logistic regression was used to obtain odds ratios for certain variables. Odds ratios estimate the probability of an event (i.e., crash) over the probability that such an event does not occur. If a variable (i.e., drug use) is not associated with a crash, the odds ratio of crash involvement associated with that variable will be 1.00. Odds ratios above 1.00 indicate a positive relationship, with stronger relationships reflected by higher odds ratios. Univariate and multivariate analyses were used to estimate the crash risk attributable to:

- Individual drugs;
- Drug classes (e.g., THC, stimulants, antidepressants);
- Drug categories (i.e., illegal drugs versus legal drugs or medications);
- Multiple drug use;
- Alcohol; and
- Combined use of alcohol and drugs.

Not all of these results are presented in this summary (see the report by Lacey et al., 2015, report in preparation).

Table 3 shows the unadjusted odds ratios for crash involvement for selected drug classes (THC, antidepressants, narcotic analgesics, sedatives and stimulants). It also shows the odds ratios for crash involvement for the two types of drugs: illegal drugs and legal (medicinal) drugs. From this table, it appears that THC is associated with a significantly elevated risk of crashing (by about 1.25 times or 25%). Similarly, the use of any illegal drugs is associated with a significant increase in the risk of crashing (by 1.21 times or 21%).

Table 3. Unadjusted Odds Ratios Between Drug Class Use and Crash Risk

Drug of Interest	Unadjusted Odds Ratio	P Value
THC (Marijuana)	1.25	0.01
Sedatives	1.30	0.06
Narcotic Analgesics	1.15	0.26
Antidepressants	1.06	0.75
Stimulants	1.01	0.40
Illegal Drugs	1.21	0.01
Legal Drugs	1.07	0.43

The risk of crash involvement for each category and class of drug is compared to the crash involvement rate for drug-negative drivers. An odds ratio of 1.00 means the crash involvement rate is the same. P Values from logistic regression (Wald Test). Shading indicates statistical significance.

These unadjusted odds ratios must be interpreted with caution as they do not account for other factors that may contribute to increased crash risk. Other factors, such as demographic variables, have been shown to have a significant effect on crash risk. For example, male drivers have a higher crash rate than female drivers. Likewise, young drivers have a higher crash rate than older drivers. To the extent that these demographic variables are correlated with specific types of drug use, they may account for some of the increased crash risk associated with drug use.

Table 4 examines the odds ratios for the same categories and classes of drugs, adjusted for the demographic variables of age, gender, and race/ethnicity. This analysis shows that the significant increased risk of crash involvement associated with THC and illegal drugs shown in Table 3 is not found after adjusting for these demographic variables. This finding suggests that these demographic variables may have co-varied with drug use and accounted for most of the increased crash risk. For example, if the THC-positive drivers were predominantly young males, their apparent crash risk may have been related to age and gender rather than use of THC.

Table 4. Adjusted Odds Ratios Between Drug Class Use and Crash Risk (Adjusted for Demographic Variables: Age, Gender And Race/Ethnicity)

Drug of Interest	Adjusted Odds Ratio	95% CI*	P Value
THC (Marijuana)	1.05	0.86 – 1.27	0.65
Antidepressants	0.87	0.57 – 1.32	0.51

Table 4. (Continued)

Drug of Interest	Adjusted Odds Ratio	95% CI*	P Value
Narcotic Analgesics	1.14	0.85 – 1.51	0.39
Sedatives	1.27	0.93 – 1.75	0.13
Stimulants	0.94	0.72 – 1.22	0.64
Illegal Drugs	1.04	0.88 – 1.23	0.65
Legal Drugs	1.03	0.84 – 1.27	0.79

The risk of crash involvement for each category and class of drug is compared to the crash involvement rate for drug-negative drivers. An odds ratio of 1.00 means the crash involvement rate is the same. *(CI = Confidence Interval).

Table 5. Adjusted Odds Ratios Between Drug Use and Crash Risk (Adjusted for Demographic Variables and Alcohol Use)

Drug of Interest	Adjusted Odds Ratio	95% CI*	P Value
THC (Marijuana)	1.00	0.83 – 1.22	0.98
Antidepressants	0.86	0.56 – 1.33	0.50
Narcotic Analgesics	1.17	0.87 – 1.56	0.30
Sedatives	1.19	0.86 – 1.64	0.29
Stimulants	0.92	0.70 – 1.19	0.51
Illegal Drugs	0.99	0.84 – 1.18	0.99
Legal Drugs	1.02	0.83 – 1.26	0.83

The risk of crash involvement for each category and class of drug is compared to the crash involvement rate for drug-negative drivers. An odds ratio of 1.00 means the crash involvement rate is the same. *(CI = Confidence Interval)

Relative Crash Risk Estimates of Drugs in Combination with Alcohol

Table 5 adjusts the odds ratios by both demographic variables and the presence of alcohol. When the effect of alcohol is removed, the odds ratios decline further (except for a non-significant increase for narcotic analgesics).

As was described above, there was no difference in crash risk for marijuana (THC)-positive drivers who were also positive for alcohol than for marijuana (THC)-positive drivers with no alcohol, beyond the risk attributable to alcohol. Further analyses examined the potential interaction between drug use and breath alcohol concentration (BrAC). No statistically significant interaction effect on crash risk was found between any drug class or drug category and BrAC level.

To further explore the relationship between alcohol and drug use on crash risk, we collapsed drug use into two categories: positive drug use or negative drug use, and collapsed alcohol use into three categories: no alcohol use, alcohol use below 0.05 BrAC and alcohol use at or above 0.05 BrAC. A BrAC of 0.05 was used for this purpose because at this level the risk of crash involvement is double that of a sober driver. Drivers who were negative for drug use and alcohol use were the reference in this conditional logistic regression analysis.

The results in Table 6 show that alcohol (≥0.05 BrAC), together with no drug presence, has the greatest effect on crash risk (shaded), raising the risk 6.75 times over that for drivers with no alcohol and no drugs. The adjusted odds ratios for alcohol levels ≥ 0.05 BrAC with drugs, and for alcohol levels ≥ 0.05 BrAC without drugs, are both significantly increased (more than 5 times higher). The relatively small difference between the odds ratio associated with alcohol levels at or above 0.05 BrAC, with and without drugs, was not statistically significant.

Table 6. Contribution of Alcohol and Drugs to Crash Risk

Drug and Alcohol Use	Adjusted Odds Ratio	95% CI*	P Value
No Alcohol ! No Drug	1.00		
No Alcohol ! Positive Drug	1.02	0.88 – 1.17	0.83
Positive Alcohol (< 0.05) ! No Drug	0.84	0.55 – 1.29	0.43
Positive Alcohol (< 0.05) Positive Drug	1.03	0.55 – 1.94	0.93
Positive Alcohol (≥ 0.05) ! No Drug	6.75	4.20 – 10.84	<0.0001
Positive Alcohol (≥ 0.05) ! Positive Drug	5.34	2.75 – 10.37	<0.0001

Shading indicates statistical significance. Reference for all conditions was no drug and no alcohol. *CI = Confidence Interval.

ALCOHOL USE IN CRASH-INVOLVED AND CONTROL DRIVERS

Table 7 shows the number and percentage of drivers using alcohol at various BrAC levels for the crash-involved and control drivers. Some 10,221 crash and control drivers provided breath samples (3,353 crash-involved drivers and 6,868 control drivers). Drivers with BrACs at or above 0.08 were clearly overrepresented in the crash population compared to the control population (2.83% of the crash-involved drivers versus 0.38% of the control drivers).

The percentage of crash-involved drivers with BrACs at or above 0.05 but below 0.08 was slightly larger than, but did not differ significantly from, the percentage of control drivers (0.54% versus 0.33%). Also, for drivers with BrACs over zero but below 0.05, there was a slightly larger, but non-significant percentage of control drivers than crash-involved drivers in this BrAC range (2.01% versus 1.64%).

The percentage of crash-involved drivers who were alcohol-positive was almost double the percentage of control drivers who were alcohol-positive (5.01% versus 2.72%).

Table 7. Percent Crash and Control Drivers Alcohol-Positive by BrAC Level (Breath Test)

	Crash		Control		
Alcohol Level	N	%	N	%	P Value
BrAC > 0.08	95	2.83%	26	0.38%	< 0.0001
BrAC ≥ 0.05 – < 0.08	18	0.54%	23	0.33%	0.13
BrAC > 0.00 – < 0.05	55	1.64%	138	2.01%	0.20
BrAC = 0.00	3,185	94.99%	6,681	97.28%	< 0.0001
All	3,353	100.00%	6,868	100.00%	
BrAC ≥ 0.05	113	3.37%	49	0.71%	< 0.0001
BrAC > 0.00	168	5.01%	187	2.72%	< 0.0001

The data in Table 7 come from all breath tested drivers, crash-involved or control, rather than only drivers who also took an oral fluid test (which is the basis for all other tables). The total number of cases in this table is slightly larger than shown in all other tables. Shading indicates statistical significance. Note: the next to last row is the combination of the first two rows, while the last row combines the first three rows.

ALCOHOL CRASH RISK ESTIMATE

An analysis was conducted to estimate the crash risk of driving at various individual BrAC levels. Table 8 shows the crash risk of alcohol-positive drivers compared to alcohol-free drivers. The second column shows the unadjusted relative risk by BrAC level, while the third column shows the relative risk adjusted for age and gender. The unadjusted risks are somewhat lower than those shown when adjusted for age and gender for alcohol levels below 0.05 BrAC. The unadjusted risk is the same at 0.06 BrAC. The unadjusted risk is higher at alcohol levels, at and above, 0.07 BrAC.

Table 8. BrAC Relative Risk Unadjusted and Adjusted for Age and Gender

BrAC	Unadjusted Risk	Adjusted Risk (Age and Gender)
0.00	1.00	1.00
0.01	0.51	0.54
0.02	0.82	0.85
0.03	1.17	1.20
0.04	1.57	1.60
0.05	2.05	2.07
0.06	2.61	2.61
0.07	3.25	3.22
0.08	3.98	3.93
0.09	4.83	4.73
0.10	5.79	5.64
0.11	6.88	6.67
0.12	8.11	7.82
0.13	9.51	9.11
0.14	11.07	10.56
0.15	12.82	12.18
0.16	14.78	13.97
0.17	16.97	15.96
0.18	19.40	18.17
0.19	22.09	20.60
0.20+	25.08	23.29

Note: (Relative to BrAC = .00)

Based on the adjusted risk, drivers with a BrAC of 0.05 are approximately 2 times more likely to crash than drivers at zero BrAC. At 0.08 BrAC the adjusted relative risk of crashing is approximately four times that of drivers at zero BrAC. At a BrAC of 0.10 the adjusted risk increases to approximately 6 times, and at 0.15 BrAC drivers are at least 12 times as likely to crash.

Case Control Study Procedure

Data was collected from more than 3,000 crash-involved drivers and 6,000 non-crash involved (control) drivers. Crash-involved drivers were recruited at the scene of police-reported crashes. In order to match characteristics of control drivers with those of crash-involved drivers as closely as possible while maintaining random selection, the non-crash involved drivers were recruited one week later at the same locations where crash-involved drivers were recruited. Two controls for each crash-involved driver were randomly selected from traffic passing the crash location, driving in the same direction of travel, on the same day of week and at the same time of day one week later. To accomplish this selection methodology, research teams operated 24 hours a day, seven days a week.

All study participants (crash-involved and control drivers) were asked for a breath alcohol test, oral fluid sample and blood sample. Participation in the study was voluntary and anonymous and met Federal standards regarding the protection of human subjects. Any subject who was unsafe to drive was provided with alternative transportation home.

Types of Crashes

It should be noted that this study included all types of police-reported crashes. Other studies have focused solely on more serious crashes (injury or fatal crashes). The survey staff responded to 2,682 crashes in which one or more crash-involved drivers participated in the survey by providing oral fluid or blood samples. Approximately one sixth (16% or 431) were single-vehicle crashes and 84 percent were multiple-vehicle crashes (n = 2,251). As shown in Table 9, 33.6 percent were crashes involving an injury (n = 886) or fatality (n = 15).

Table 9. Types of Crashes

Type of Crash	Number	Percent
All Crashes	2,682	100.0%
Fatal	15	0.6%
Injury	886	33.0%
Property Damage	1,781	66.4%

Study Participants and Participation Rates

The 2,682 crashes noted above resulted in 3,887 eligible crash-involved drivers (ineligible drivers included drivers of commercial vehicles, drivers too impaired to give informed consent, drivers under age 18, and drivers with language barriers). One week later, 7,397 eligible control drivers were identified. Of the eligible crash-involved drivers 3,682 provided informed consent to participate in the study and 7,176 of the eligible control drivers provided informed consent to participate (see Table 10). This represented an overall 96.2% participation rate. Most of these drivers (90.6%) agreed to take a breath test (86.3% or 3,353 of the crash-involved drivers and 92.8% or 6,868 of the control drivers). Finally, 82.3 percent of the eligible drivers provided an oral fluid sample (79.6% of the crash-involved drivers and 83.7% of the control drivers). Only crash-involved drivers for whom two matched control drivers were obtained were included in the crash risk analyses.

Table 10. Number of Participants and Participation Rates

	Crash-Involved	Control	Total
Drivers	Number (%)	Number (%)	Number (%)
Eligible	3,887	7,397	11,284
Participated	3,682 (94.7%)	7,176 (97.0%)	10,858 (96.2%)
Breath Test	3,353 (86.3%)	6,868 (92.8%)	10,221 (90.6%)
Oral Fluid	3,095 (79.6%)	6,190 (83.7%)	9,285 (82.3%)

Participation rates based on the percentage of eligible crash-involved and control drivers. The numbers and percentages shown for drivers providing a breath test or oral fluid sample include only crash-involved and control drivers where two control drivers participated who matched a participating crash-involved driver.

Consistency with Previous Research Findings

Findings from this study corroborate those from other important studies in several key aspects, adding further assurance that this study sample was not unusual or highly biased in some unknown fashion. In particular, the findings from this study regarding the prevalence of alcohol and drug use by drivers reflect recent findings from NHTSA's 2007 National Roadside Survey of Alcohol and Drug Use by Drivers, and findings from this study regarding the crash risks of drivers at various Breath Alcohol (BrAC) levels reflect those of prior alcohol crash risk analyses.

Comparison with Results from the 2007 National Roadside Survey of Alcohol and Drug Use by Drivers

In 2007, NHTSA conducted the fourth decennial roadside survey of alcohol use by drivers. The 2007 survey also collected information on drivers' use of a wide variety of potentially impairing drugs. The survey provided nationally representative information on the prevalence of alcohol and drug use by drivers (Compton & Berning, 2009; Lacey et al., 2009). As shown in Table 11, the 2007 survey showed that 9.7 percent of all drivers tested were alcohol-positive (based on a breath test), while 13.6 percent were drug-positive (based on an oral fluid test). The current study found a much smaller percentage of drivers tested (during similar hours used for data collection in the 2007 roadside survey) who were alcohol positive (2.9%), while a slightly larger 14.4 percent of the control drivers were drug-positive (Table 11).

The differences between the two studies in the proportion of drivers found to be alcohol-positive are likely to have resulted from the concentration of Roadside Survey data collection on weekend nighttime hours, while this study included data from all days of the week and all hours of the day. For example, in the 2007 Roadside Survey the percentage of alcohol-positive weekday daytime drivers was only 1.0 percent, while on weekend nights 12.4 percent of the drivers were alcohol-positive. In this study, 1.9 percent of weekday daytime drivers were alcohol- positive, while 9.4 percent of weekend nighttime drivers were alcohol-positive.

In terms of THC use, the 2007 Roadside Survey found 7.7 percent of weekend nighttime drivers were positive for THC, while, in this study, 9.4 percent of the weekend nighttime control drivers were positive for THC. Both studies showed a similar pattern in which THC use on weekend nights appear to be almost double the daytime use rate.

The higher drug prevalence rate at nighttime strongly suggests that recreational use is a significant component of overall drug use. Medical drug use would not be expected to differ between day and night, nor weekday or weekend. In addition, a comparison of the distribution of THC concentrations between the two studies showed generally similar distributions.

Table 11. Comparison of the Weekend Nighttime and Weekday Daytime Alcohol, Drug and Marijuana (THC) Prevalence Between the 2007 NRS and Crash Risk Control Drivers (Breath Test and Oral Fluid Test)

Substance	2007 NRS	Crash Risk Controls
Alcohol Positive	9.7%	2.9%
Alcohol Positive Nighttime	12.4%	9.4%
Alcohol Positive Daytime	1.0%	1.9%
Alcohol ≥ 0.08	1.7%	0.4%
Alcohol ≥ 0.08 Nighttime	2.2%	2.1%
Alcohol ≥ 0.08 Daytime	0.1%	0.1%
Drug Positive	13.6%	14.4%
Drug Positive Nighttime	14.4%	18.4%
Drug Positive Daytime	11.0%	14.6%
THC (Marijuana) Positive	6.9%	6.1%
THC (Marijuana) Nighttime	7.7%	9.4%
THC (Marijuana) Daytime	4.5%	5.4%

Note: Weekend Nighttime drivers refers to drivers from Friday and Saturday nights from 10 p.m. – midnight and 1 a.m. – 3 a.m. for the 2007 National Roadside Survey, and 9 p.m. to 3 a.m. for the control drivers from this crash risk study. Weekday Daytime refers to 9:30 a.m. – 11:30 a.m. and 1:30 p.m. – 3:30 p.m. for the 2007 National Roadside Survey and 9 a.m. – 3 p.m. for the control drivers from this crash risk study.

COMPARISON WITH PRIOR ALCOHOL RELATIVE CRASH RISK ESTIMATES

A considerable body of research has demonstrated the impairing effects of alcohol on driving-related skills. The relationship between BAC and crash risk was first well established by the "Grand Rapids Study" in 1964 (Borkenstein et al., 1964). That study provided compelling evidence that even moderate BAC levels were associated with increased crash risk and that the risk grew rapidly at BACs of .10 or higher. A study by NHTSA in the late 1990s provided more precise estimates of the risk of driving at lower BrACs (Blomberg, Peck, Moskowitz, Burns & Florentino, 2005).

To compare the findings of this study with the existing body of evidence regarding alcohol crash risk, analyses similar to those used in earlier studies were performed using data collected from this current study. These analyses compare the crash risk of alcohol-positive drivers with those of alcohol-free drivers (zero BrAC). This comparison provides a good indication whether this new study's sample was consistent with previous studies, and is useful as an indicator of any possible bias in the sample. The analyses also compare the crash risk of alcohol-positive drivers with those of alcohol-free drivers (zero BrAC) among those drivers who tested negative for drugs.

The results of the comparison showed a high degree of consistency with prior results and therefore suggest that the sample utilized in this study was comparable to those of prior studies. We compared the relative risk by BrAC level for the subjects in this study (calculated using the model used by Blomberg) with the relative risk curve from the Blomberg et al. (2005) study and found no significant difference between studies. The model presented above in Table 8 is slightly different from the Blomberg model, but fits the data better. There are some differences in risk estimates between the model presented in Table 8 and the Blomberg model. For example, at a 0.04 BrAC our model estimated the relative risk at 1.60 versus 1.00 for the Blomberg model, while at a 0.10 BrAC the estimates were 5.64 for our model and 2.66 for the Blomberg model. The risk estimates from this study were, for the most part, higher than those in the Blomberg study but they were for the most part within the 95-percent confidence limits.

SUMMARY AND DISCUSSION

This study of crash risk found a statistically significant increase in unadjusted crash risk for drivers who tested positive for use of illegal drugs (1.21 times), and THC specifically (1.25 times). However, analyses incorporating adjustments for age, gender, ethnicity, and alcohol concentration level did not show a significant increase in levels of crash risk associated with the presence of drugs. This finding indicates that these other variables (age, gender ethnicity and alcohol use) were highly correlated with drug use and account for much of the increased risk associated with the use of illegal drugs and with THC.

This study found a statistically significant association between driver alcohol level and crash risk both before and after adjustment for demographic factors. These findings were generally consistent with similar analyses conducted in prior crash risk studies. Findings from this study indicate that crash risk grows exponentially with increasing BrAC. The study shows that at low levels of alcohol (e.g., 0.03 BrAC) the risk of crashing is increased by 20 percent, at moderate alcohol levels (0.05 BrAC) risk increases to double that of sober drivers, and at a higher level (0.10 BrAC) the risk increases to five and a half times. At a BrAC of 0.15, the risk is 12 times, and by BrACs of 0.20+ the risk is over 23 times higher.

This is the first large-scale case control study in the United States to assess the crash risks associated with both drug and alcohol use by drivers. Findings from this study provide valuable insights concerning the current nature of the impaired driving problem. However, considering the complexity of the impaired driving issue, especially concerning use of drugs other than alcohol, and the challenges of obtaining relevant information on this topic, these findings should be viewed in the context of the established body of scientific evidence on the subject.

Strengths of this study include the large number of crashes in the sample, the care taken in matching control subjects to the crash-involved driver sample, and the consistency in data resulting from rigorous adherence to data collection procedures and analytical methods. Inherent limitations of such a study design include a localized sample of crashes with unknown generalizability, and a bias toward less severe crashes. These limitations are primarily the result of practical constraints presented by available time and financial resources. It is possible that the findings could have differed if data were collected in another location or if there had been additional severe crashes.

The Blomberg study of alcohol crash risk used data collected on both coasts of the United States and did not find a significant difference between sites. Also a sample less representative of crashes across the country (in which most crashes are property damage crashes with a smaller number of injury crashes and an even smaller number of fatal crashes), that was restricted to only serious injury and fatal crashes, would undoubtedly result in a greater percentage of drivers with higher BrAC levels, and possibly higher drug levels.

In the background and introduction section (above) we reviewed previous studies that have estimated the risk of crash involvement associated with marijuana use by drivers. The results of this study are In line with the previous research on the effects of marijuana on the risk of crash involvement. While a number of previous studies have shown some increased risk associated with marijuana use by drivers, many studies have not found increased risk. As was noted previously, studies that measure the presence of THC in the drivers' blood or oral fluid, rather than relying on self-report tend to have much lower (or no elevated) crash risk estimates. Likewise, better controlled studies have found lower (or no) elevated crash risk estimates. Thus, the results of this study are consistent with the previous well controlled studies.

While the findings of this case control study were equivocal with regard to the crash risk associated with drug use by drivers, these results do not indicate that drug use by drivers is risk-free. The study limitations cited above, together with the findings of numerous other studies using different and complementary methods, need to be carefully considered before more definitive conclusions about drug use and crash risk can be reached.

The findings of this study notwithstanding, the established body of scientific evidence on the subject of drug impairment indicates that in some situations, drugs other than alcohol can seriously impair driving ability. This study provides further confirmation that driver impairment is a very serious safety concern and that it is involves a very certain element of alcohol impairment and a less-certain element of drug impairment. The 2007 National Roadside Survey of Alcohol and Drug Use by Drivers indicates the prevalence of drivers with levels of alcohol at or above the illegal per se limit of .08 BrAC has declined sharply over the past several decades. Such trend information regarding drug use by drivers is not yet available. However, recent policy changes regarding the medicinal and recreational use of marijuana suggest that further monitoring and research in this area are critical for public safety. NHTSA plans to release the results of a recent study, the 2013–2014 National Roadside Survey of Alcohol and Drug Use by Drivers, this month which will for the first time contain trend Information on drug use by drivers.

Background on Drug Use and Driving

This case control study contributes to a better understanding of the nature and scope of the drugged driving problem. From a public health perspective, relatively little is known about the contribution of drugs other than alcohol to traffic crashes. Understanding the effects of other drugs on driving is considerably more complicated than is the case for alcohol impairment. This stems from the fact that there are many potentially impairing drugs and the relationship between dosage levels and driving impairment is complex and uncertain in many cases. Additional challenges include the large differences among individuals with regard to response to the same dose of many drugs, and differences in impairment resulting from acute versus chronic use of some drugs.

Many drugs have been shown to impair driving related skills in laboratory dosing studies. Simulator studies, and closed-course driving studies employing psychomotor tasks like vigilance, reaction time, divided attention tasks, cognitive and executive functions, car following, lane keeping, speed control, and emergency maneuvers have shown reductions in driving-related functions due to drug effects. Individual drugs or drug combinations produce different impairing effects that are likely to increase the risk of crashing in various ways. For example, some may produce risk-taking behaviors, while others may reduce visual scanning, result in poor judgment, or lead to inattention.

For More Information

For questions regarding the information presented in this document, please contact Amy Berning at amy.berning@dot.gov.

Detailed information about the study design and results will be available in a technical report to be released in the near future (see Lacey, J.H., Kelley-Baker, T., Berning, A., Romano, E., Ramirez, A., Yao, J. Moore, C. Brainard, K., Carr, K., and Pell, K. (2015, report in preparation). Alcohol and Drug Crash Risk: A Case Control Study, Washington, DC: National Highway Traffic Safety Administration).

References

Abridge, M., Hayden, J. A., Cartwright, J. L. (2012). Acute Cannabis Consumption and Motor Vehicle Collision Risk: A Systemic Review of Observational Studies and Meta-Analysis. *BJM*, http://dx.doi.org/10.1136/bjm.e536.

Blomberg, R. D., Peck, R. C., Moskowitz, H., Burns, M. & Fiorentino, D. (2005). Crash Risk of Alcohol Involved Driving: A Case-Control Study, Final Report to the National Highway Traffic Safety Administration. Stamford, CT: Dunlap and Associates, Inc.

Blomberg, R. D., Peck, R. C., Moskowitz, H., Burns, M., & Fiorentino, D. (2009). The Long Beach/Fort Lauderdale Relative Risk Study. *Journal of Safety Research*, 40, 285–292.

Borkenstein, R. F., Crowther, R. F., Shumate, R. P., Zeil, W. B., & Zylman, R. (1964). The Role of the Drinking Driver in Traffic Accidents.

Bloomington, IN: Department of Police Administration, Indiana University.

Borkenstein, R. F., Crowther, R. F., Shumate, R. P., Ziel, W. B., & Zylman, R. (1974). The Role of the Drinking Driver in Traffic Accidents: The Grand Rapids Study. Blutalkohol, 11, Supplement 1, 1–132.

Compton, R. P., Vegega, M. E., & Smither, D. (2009). Drug-Impaired Driving: Understanding the Problem and Ways to Reduce It, A Report to Congress. (Report No. DOT HS 811 268). Washington, DC: National Highway Traffic Safety Administration.

DuPont, R. L., Voas, R. B., Walsh, J. M., Shea, C., Talpins, S. K., & Neil, N. M. (2012). The Need for Drugged Driving Per Se Laws: A Commentary. *Traffic Injury Prevention*, 13(1), 31–42.

Elvik, R. (2013). Risk of Road Accident Associated with the Use of Drugs: A Systematic Review and Meta-analysis of Evidence from Epidemiological Studies. *Accident Analysis & Prevention*, 60, 254–267.

Hartman, R. I. & Huestis, M. A. (2013). Cannabis Effects on Driving Skills. *Clinical Chemistry*, 59(3), 478–492.

Hels, T., Bernhoft, I. M., Lyckegaard, A., Houwing, S., Hagenzieker, M., Legrand, S.A., Isaberti, C., Van der Linden, T. & Verstraete, A. (2011). Risk of Injury by Driving with Alcohol and Other Drugs. DRUID – Driving Under the Influence of Drugs, Alcohol and Medicines, D2.3.5. Available from http://www.druid-project.eu/.

Houwing, S. (2013). Estimating the Risk of Driving Under the Influence of Psychoactive Substances. University of Groningen, ISBN: 978-90-7394601901.

ICADTS. (2007). Tallories Report. Guidelines for Drugged Driving Research. International Council on Alcohol, Drugs and Traffic Safety.

Jones, R. K., Shinar, D., & Walsh, J. M. (2003). State of Knowledge of Drug-Impaired Driving. (Report No. DOT HS 809 642). Washington, DC: National Highway Traffic Safety Administration.

Lacey, J. H., Kelley-Baker, K., Furr-Holden, D., Brainard, K., & Moore, C. (2007). Pilot Test of New Roadside Survey Methodology for Impaired Driving. (Report No. DOT HS 810 704). Washington, DC: National Highway Traffic Safety Administration.

Lacey, J. H., Kelley-Baker, T., Furr-Holden, D., Voas, R. B., Moore, C., Brainard, K., Tippetts, A. S., Romano, E., Torres, P. & Berning, A. (2009). 2007 National Roadside Survey of Alcohol and Drug Use by Drivers: Methodology. (Report No. DOT HS 811 237). Washington, DC: National Highway Traffic Safety Administration.

Lacey, J. H., Kelley-Baker, T., Furr-Holden, D., Voas, R. B., Romano, E., Ramirez, A., Brainard, K., Moore, C., Torres, P., & Berning, A. (2009). 2007 National Roadside Survey of Alcohol and Drug Use by Drivers: Drug Results (Report No. DOT HS 811 249). Washington, DC: National Highway Traffic Safety Administration.

Lacey, J. H., Kelley-Baker, T., Furr-Holden, D., Voas, R. B., Romano, E., Torres, P., Tippetts, A.S., Ramirez, A., Brainard,K., & Berning,A. (2009, December). 2007National Roadside Survey of Alcohol and Drug Use by Drivers: Alcohol Results (Report No. DOT HS 811 248). Washington, DC: National Highway Traffic Safety Administration.

Lia, G., Bradya, J. E., & Chen, Q. (2013). Drug Use and Fatal Motor Vehicle Crashes: A Case-Control Study. *Accident Analysis and Prevention*, 60, 205–210.

Lund, A. K., & Wolfe, A. C. (1991). Changes in the Incidence of Alcohol-Impaired Driving in the United States, 1973– 1986. *Journal of Studies on Alcohol*, 52(4), 293–301.

Moskowitz, H. (1995). Marijuana and Driving. *Accident Analysis and Prevention*, 17: 323–345.

Robbe, H. W. J., & O'Hanlon, J. F. (1993). Marijuana and Actual Driving Performance. (Report No. DOT HS 808 078). Washington, DC: U.S. Department of Transportation.

Romano, E., Torres-Saavedra, P., Voas, R. B. & Lacey, J. H. (2014). Drugs and Alcohol: Their Relative Crash Risk. *Journal of Studies on Alcohol and Drugs*, pp 1–9.

Terhune, K. W. (1982). The Role of Alcohol, Marijuana and Other Drugs in the Accidents of Injured Drivers. Volume 1: Findings. (Report No. DOT HS 806 199). Washington, DC: National Highway Traffic Safety Administration.

Terhune, K. W., Ippolito, C. A., Hendricks, D. L., Michalovic, J. G., Bogema, S. C., Santinga, P. (1992). The Incidence and Role of Drugs in Fatally Injured Drivers. (Report No. DOT HS 808 065). Washington, DC: U.S. Department of Transportation.

Voas, R. B., Wells, J., Lestina, D., Williams, A., & Greene, M. (1998). Drinking and Driving in the United States: The 1996 National Roadside Survey. *Accident Analysis and Prevention*, 30(2), 267–275.

Wash, J. M., Flegel, R., Atkins, R., (2005). Drug and Alcohol Use Among Drivers Admitted to a Level-1 Trauma Center. *Accident Analysis and Prevention*, 37(5), 894–901.

Wolfe, A. C. (1974). 1973 US National Roadside Breath Testing Survey: Procedures and Results. Ann Arbor, MI: University of Michigan Highway Safety Research Institute.

In: Drug-Impaired Driving
Editor: Tobias H. Erickson

ISBN: 978-1-63482-871-0

Chapter 3

RESULTS OF THE 2013–2014 NATIONAL ROADSIDE SURVEY OF ALCOHOL AND DRUG USE BY DRIVERS*

Amy Berning, Richard Compton and Kathryn Wochinger

Over the last four decades, the National Highway Traffic Safety Administration and/or the Insurance Institute for Highway Safety (IIHS) conducted four national surveys to estimate the prevalence of drinking and driving in the United States (Wolfe, 1974; Lund & Wolfe, 1991; Voas et al, 1998; Compton & Berning, 2009; Lacey et al, 2009). The first National Roadside Survey (NRS) was conducted in 1973, followed by national surveys of drivers in 1986, 1996, 2007, and now 2013–2014. These surveys used a stratified random sample of weekend nighttime drivers in the contiguous 48 States and collected data directly from drivers on the road.

The 2007 NRS added procedures to the NRS for the first time to estimate the use by drivers of other potentially impairing drugs. Prior roadside surveys had only collected breath samples to determine breath alcohol concentration (BrAC). Due to developments in analytical toxicology, NHTSA determined it would be feasible in the 2007 and 2013–2014 surveys to determine driver use of a variety of potentially impairing drugs including illegal drugs as well as legal medications.

* This is an edited, reformatted and augmented version of a Traffic Safety Facts Research Note, Report No. DOT HS 812 118, issued by the National Highway Traffic Safety Administration, Office of Behavioral Safety Research, February 2015.

In 2013–2014, the National Highway Traffic Safety Administration conducted the most recent National Roadside Survey of Alcohol and Drug Use by Drivers.[1] This voluntary and anonymous study is the second to collect data on drug use, presenting our first opportunity to examine drug use trends on a national scale. The 2013– 2014 NRS was designed to produce national estimates of alcohol and drug use by weekday daytime and weekend nighttime drivers. Thus, the use rates presented below are national prevalence rates calculated from the percentage of drivers using alcohol or drugs and adjusted with an appropriate weighting scheme.

SUMMARY OF RESULTS

Prevalence of Alcohol Use by Drivers

The NRS surveys reveal a decreasing trend in alcohol use from the first survey in 1973 to the most recent one in 2013– 2014. Figure 1 shows the percentage of weekend nighttime drivers with BrACs across three categories: BrAC of .005 to .049 g/210 L;[2] BrACs of .050 to .079; and BrACs of .080 and higher. The surveys found a decline in each BrAC category. Further, there has been a large decrease in the percentage of drivers who were alcohol positive, from 35.9 percent in 1973 to 8.3 percent in 2013–2014. For BrACs of .08 and higher, there was a decrease from 7.5 percent in 1973 to 1.5 percent in 2013–2014, revealing an impressive 80 percent reduction in the percentage of alcohol-impaired drivers on the road on weekend nights. Also of importance is the decrease from 6.1 percent to 1.6 percent from 1973 to 2013–2014 for BrACs of .050 to .079 category.

The 2013–2014 survey found large differences by the day of week and the time of day in the likelihood of drivers being alcohol positive or having an illegal BrAC (Table 1). During weekday daytime hours (Friday), only 1.1 percent of drivers were alcohol positive, while at weekend nighttime hours (Friday and Saturday), 8.3 percent of drivers were alcohol positive. During weekday daytime hours there were very few drivers with illegal BrACs (BrAC $\geq$ .08), just 0.4 percent, while at weekend nighttime hours 1.5 percent drivers had illegal BrACs. Daytime compared to nighttime percentages are statistically significant. Compared with the NRS 2007, the 2013–2014 NRS BrAC prevalence shown in Figure 1 was significantly lower only for the .005 to .049 BrAC category.

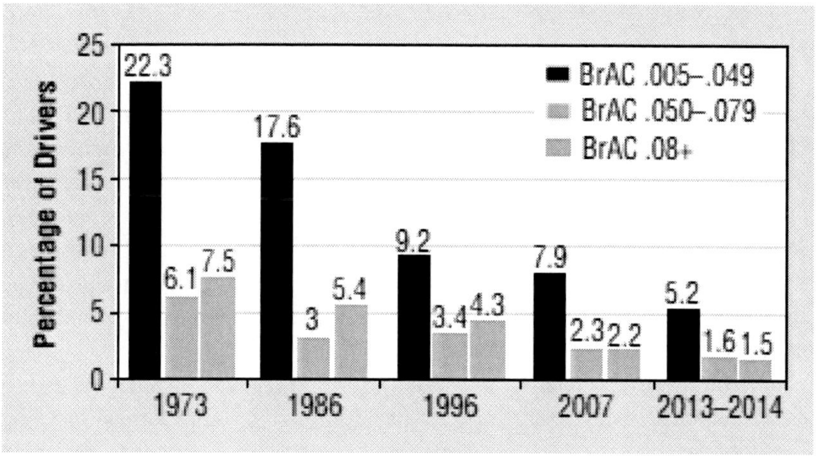

Figure 1. Percentage of Weekend Nighttime Drivers by BrAC Category in the Five National Roadside Surveys.[3]

Table 1. Alcohol Prevalence by Data Collection Period and BrAC in the 2013–2014 NRS

Data Collection Time Period	% Alcohol Positive (%BrAC > .005)	% BrAC > .08
Weekday Daytime	1.1%	0.4%
Weekend Nighttime	8.3%	1.5%

Prevalence of Drug Use by Drivers

The 2013–2014 study examined the use of drugs, focusing on drugs with the potential to impair driving skills, including over-the-counter, prescription, and illegal drugs.

Participants were asked to provide an oral fluid and blood sample in addition to a breath sample. The oral fluid and blood samples were tested for the presence of a large number of potentially impairing drugs including cannabinoids, stimulants, sedatives, antidepressants, and narcotic analgesics. Not all drivers provided both an oral fluid and blood sample; some drivers provided just one sample but many provided both.

The reader is cautioned that drug presence does not necessarily imply impairment. For many drug substances, drug presence can be detected after impairment that might affect driving has passed. For example, traces of marijuana use can be detected in blood samples several weeks after heavy chronic users stop ingestion. In this study, for marijuana, we tested only for THC (delta 9 tetrahydrocannabinol), the psychoactive substance in marijuana, and 11-OH-THC, its active metabolite. When marijuana is smoked or ingested, THC is absorbed into the blood stream and is distributed into areas of the body, including the brain. There are over 100 marijuana metabolites detectable in blood that research has not associated with the psychoactive effects of marijuana use. Whereas the impairment effects for various concentration levels of alcohol in the blood or breath are well understood, there is little evidence available to link concentrations of other drugs to driver performance.

Table 2. Overall Drug Prevalence by Data Collection Period and Type of Test in the 2013–2014 NRS

Time of Day	% Drug-Positive Oral Fluid Test	% Drug-Positive Blood Test	% Drug-Positive Oral Fluid and/or Blood Test
Weekday Daytime	19.0%	21.6%	22.4%
Weekend Nighttime	19.8%	21.2%	22.5%

In contrast to alcohol use, overall drug prevalence (shown in Table 2), did not appear to differ between daytime and nighttime, regardless of whether oral fluid or blood tests were conducted. The much higher nighttime use of alcohol appears to represent recreational use. For other drugs, a different pattern emerges.

As shown in Table 3, the pattern of drug use among drivers varies by day and category of drug. The prevalence of illegal drug use increases from daytime to nighttime, but there is a countervailing pattern of a reduction in prevalence of driver use of medicinal drugs in nighttime drivers compared to daytime drivers.[4]

Table 3. Drug Prevalence by Data Collection Period, Drug Category, and Type of Drug Test in the 2013–2014 NRS

Drug Category	Oral Fluid Test		Blood Test		Oral Fluid and/or Blood Test	
	N	%	N	%	N	%
Weekday Daytime						
Any Illegal Drug[5]	189	10.6%	137	11.3%	221	12.1%
Only Medications[6]						
(prescription and over-the-counter)	197	8.4%	128	10.3%	234	10.3%
Weekend Nighttime						
Any Illegal Drug	783	13.9%	423	14.3%	852	15.2%
Only Medications						
(prescription and over-the-counter)	317	5.9%	216	6.9%	391	7.3%

Table 4. Weekend Nighttime Drug Prevalence by Drug Category and Test Type Comparing 2007 Data to 2013–2014 Comparable Data

	2007 Data						2013–2014 Comparable Data					
Drug	Oral Fluid Test		Blood Test		Oral Fluid and/or Blood Test		Oral Fluid Test		Blood Test		Oral Fluid and/or Blood Test	
Category	N	%	N	%	N	%	N	%	N	%	N	%
Any Illegal Drug	635	11.4%	297	9.8%	699	12.4%	779	13.8%	422	14.3%	849	15.1%
Only Medications (prescription and over-the-counter)	201	3.0%	169	4.0%	277	3.9%	211	3.9%	155	4.9%	266	4.9%

Comparison of Drug Prevalence between the 2007 NRS and 2013–2014 NRS

The specific drugs and detection thresholds changed somewhat between the 2007 NRS and 2013–2014 NRS. A few drugs that were either not detected or rarely detected in the 2007 NRS were not included on the 2013–2014 NRS, and a few new drugs were added in the 2013–2014 NRS. For example, we tested for selected synthetic cannabinoids in the new survey. Also, improvements in analytical technology allowed the detection thresholds to be lowered significantly for a number of drugs in the 2013–2014 NRS. To compare the prevalence rates between the 2007 NRS and 2013–2014 NRS, we included only the drugs that were tested for in both surveys and based 2013–2014 NRS prevalence rates using the cutoff levels from the 2007 NRS.

To account for these refinements in lab testing since 2007, Table 4 presents the 2013–2014 NRS data after applying the same set of drugs and drug cutoff levels as used for 2007 survey. The results from either oral fluid tests or blood tests, or both oral fluid and/or blood tests, show a small increase in drug-positive drivers using medications (from 3.9% in 2007 to 4.9% in 2013–2014), and a larger increase in the prevalence of illegal drugs (from 12.4% in 2007 to 15.1% in 2013–2014). In 2007, 16.3 percent of weekend nighttime drivers were drug-positive based on the combined results of either or both oral fluid and blood tests (Compton & Berning, 2009). In 2013–2014, 20.0 percent of weekend nighttime drivers tested positive for drugs using the 2007 cut-off criteria.

The drug with the largest increase in weekend nighttime prevalence was THC (Table 5). In the 2007 NRS, 8.6 percent of weekend nighttime drivers tested positive for THC (based on the combined oral fluid and/or blood tests), whereas in the 2013–2014 NRS, 12.6 percent of weekend nighttime drivers tested positive for THC, a 48 percent increase.

Changes in State policy on marijuana use, including medical and recreational use, may have contributed to an increase in marijuana use by drivers. However, the survey does not permit a state-by-state comparison. The change in use may reflect the emergence of a new trend in the country that warrants monitoring.

Survey Methodology

This most recent NRS started in the summer of 2013, continued through the spring of 2014, and involved 60 sites across the contiguous United States. The study used a multistage sampling procedure based on the National Automotive Sampling System—General Estimates System (NHTSA, 2008). The sites were large cities, counties, or groups of counties representing four regions within the United States and three levels of population density. As a whole, the 60 sites provide a representative sample of drivers across the country. The 2013–2014 NRS attempted to re-visit the same sites as 2007; however, because not all sites were available, statistical sampling techniques were used to identify replacement sites with similar characteristics.

Roadside survey data were collected in 5 different locations at each site (for a total of 300 locations). Although there were practical considerations for selecting a site, such as traffic flow and safety, the 5 locations were randomly chosen within the boundaries of the cooperating local law enforcement agency's area of jurisdiction. This approach provided, as much as possible, a representative sample of drivers for that site. Locations were not selected on the basis of assumptions of where there would be a high percentage of alcohol- or drug-positive drivers. The objective of this study was to estimate the alcohol and other drug prevalence of all drivers "on the road in the United States" during the given time periods.

Table 5. Weekend Nighttime Prevalence of THC in 2007 Compared to 2013–2014 Comparable Data

2007 Data						2013–2014 Comparable Data					
Oral Fluid Test		Blood Test		Oral Fluid and/or Blood Test		Oral Fluid Test		Blood Test		Oral Fluid and/or Blood Test	
N	%	N	%	N	%	N	%	N	%	N	%
438	7.7%	234	7.6%	499	8.6%	597	11.3%	332	11.7%	663	12.6%

In the 2007 NRS, in an effort to learn more about the presence of alcohol and drug use during daytime driving, we added data collection on Fridays during the day, from either 9:30 to 11:30 a.m., or 1:30 to 3:30 p.m. (the times were randomized across sites). This additional data collection allowed us to examine drug use and alcohol trends among daytime drivers. This method was repeated for the 2013–2014 NRS, and data were collected on weekend nights, from 10:00 p.m. to midnight, and from 1 to 3 a.m. on Fridays (i.e., early Saturday mornings) and from 1 to 3 a.m. on Saturdays (i.e., early Sunday mornings). By using these same time frames for each NRS, we can compare data on BrACs and drug use over time.

Participation in the survey was entirely voluntary and anonymous. When a data collector was available, drivers were allowed to enter the data collection location. Where researchers described the project and offered incentives for participation. Drivers were informed that participation was voluntary and that they were free to leave at any time. Data collectors asked participants for a breath test, an oral fluid sample, and a blood sample. The vast majority of eligible drivers entering the research area participated in the study (see Table 6). The number of drivers who entered the site and were eligible to participate (e.g., non-commercial drivers 16 and older, English- or Spanish-speaking) was 11,100. Out of the 11,100 eligible drivers, 85.2 percent (9,455 drivers) provided breath samples; 71 percent (7,881 drivers) provided oral fluid samples; and 42.2 percent (4,686 drivers) provided blood samples.

National prevalence rates were derived from a complex weighting scheme based on the volume of serious crashes at each site and the probability of a survey driver being randomly selected from the total driving trips at that site.

Table 6. Number of Participants and Participation Rates in the 2013–2014 NRS

	Participants	
Drivers	N	%
Eligible and Entered Site	11,100	100.0%
Breath Test	9,455	85.2%
Oral Fluid Test	7,881	71.0%
Blood Test	4,686	42.2%
Oral Fluid and/or Blood	7,898	71.2%

CHALLENGES IN DETERMINING HOW DRUGS AFFECT DRIVING

Most psychoactive drugs are chemically complex molecules, whose absorption, action, and elimination from the body are difficult to predict, and considerable differences exist between individuals with regard to the rates with which these processes occur. Alcohol, in comparison, is more predictable. A strong relationship between alcohol concentration and impairment has been established, as has the correlation between alcohol concentration and crash risk.

Factors that make similar prediction difficult for most other psychoactive drugs include:

- The large number of different drugs that would need to be tested (extensive testing of alcohol has been undertaken over many decades, whereas relatively little similar testing has occurred for most other drugs).

- Poor correlation between the effects on psychomotor, behavioral, and/or executive functions and blood or plasma drug concentrations (peak psychomotor, behavioral, and executive function effects do not necessarily correspond to peak blood levels; detectable blood levels may persist beyond the impairing effects or the impairing effects may be measurable when the drug cannot be detected in the blood).
- Sensitivity and tolerance (accentuation and diminution of the impairing effects with repeated exposure).
- Individual differences in absorption, distribution, action, and metabolism (some individuals will show evidence of impairment at drug concentrations that are not associated with impairment in others; wide ranges of drug concentrations in different individuals have been associated with equivalent levels of impairment).
- Accumulation (blood levels of some drugs or their metabolites may accumulate with repeated administrations if the time-course of elimination is insufficient to reduce or remove the drug or metabolite before the next dose is administered).
- Acute versus chronic administration (it is not unusual to observe greater impairment during initial administrations of drugs than is observed when the drug is administered over a long period of time).

At the current time, specific drug concentration levels cannot be reliably equated with a specific degree of driver impairment.

For More Information

For questions on this document, please contact Amy Berning at amy.berning@dot.gov.

Detailed information about the study and results will be available in upcoming publications. Three technical reports are under development: one provides a complete description of the methodology used (sampling, analysis, weighting, and imputation procedures) and subject participation rates (report entitled, 2013–2014 National Roadside Survey of Alcohol and Drug Use: Methodology). Detailed information on the use of alcohol by drivers and the relationship of alcohol to various factors like time of day and vehicle type will be available in a report entitled, 2013–2014 National Roadside Survey of Alcohol and Drug Use: Alcohol Prevalence Rates. Detailed information on the use of drugs by drivers and the combined use of drugs and alcohol, as well as more detailed trend analysis examining changes in drug prevalence from 2007 to 2013–2014 will be provided in a third report titled 2013–2014 National Roadside Survey of Alcohol and Drug Use: Drug Prevalence Rates. These upcoming reports will be posted on NHTSA's Web site.

REFERENCES

Compton, R., & Berning, A. (2009). Results of the 2007 National Roadside Survey of Alcohol and Drug Use by Drivers (Report No. DOT HS 811 175). Washington, DC: National Highway Traffic Safety Administration. Available at www.nhtsa.gov/DOT/NHTSA/Traffic%20Injury%20 Control /Articles/Associated%20Files/811175.pdf.

Lacey, J. H., Kelley-Baker, T., Furr-Holden, D., Voas, R. B., Moore, C., Brainard, K., ... & Berning, A. (2009, December). 2007 National Roadside Survey of Alcohol and Drug Use by Drivers: Methodology. (Report No. DOT HS 811 237). Washington, DC: National Highway Traffic Safety Administration. Available at www.nhtsa.gov/ staticfiles/nti/pdf/ 811237. pdf.

Lacey, J. H., Kelley-Baker, T., Furr-Holden, D., Voas, R. B., Romano, E., Ramirez, A., ... & Berning, A. (2009, December). 2007 National Roadside Survey of Alcohol and Drug Use by Drivers: Drug Results (Report No. DOT HS 811 249). Washington, DC: National Highway Traffic Safety Administration. Available at www.nhtsa.gov/ DOT/NHTSA/ Traffic% 20Injury%20Control/Articles/ Associated%20Files/811249.pdf.

Lacey, J. H., Kelley-Baker, T., Furr-Holden, D., Voas, R. B., Romano, E., Torres, P., ... & Berning, A. (2009, December). 2007 National Roadside Survey of Alcohol and Drug Use by Drivers: Alcohol Results (Report No. DOT HS 811 248). Washington, D.C: National Highway Traffic Safety Administration. Available at ntl.bts.gov/ lib/31000/31600/31643/ 811248. pdf.

Lund, A. K., & Wolfe, A. C. (1991). Changes in the incidence of alcohol-impaired driving in the United States, 1973- 1986. *Journal of Studies on Alcohol*, 52(4), 293–301.

NHTSA. (2008). National Automotive Sampling System Brochure (Report No. DOT HS 807 304). Washington, D.C: National Highway Traffic

Safety Administration. Available at www.nhtsa.gov/DOT/NHTSA/NCSA/Content/PDF/NASSbrochure.pdf.

Voas, R. B., Wells, J., Lestina, D., Williams, A., & Greene, M. (1998). Drinking and driving in the United States: The 1996 National Roadside Survey. *Accident Analysis and Prevention*, 30(2), 267–275.

Wolfe, A. C. (1974). 1973 US National Roadside Breath Testing Survey: Procedures and Results. Ann Arbor, MI: University of Michigan Safety Research Institute.

End Notes

[1] The Office of National Drug Control Policy provided funds to NHTSA for this study. The National Institute on Drug Abuse, and the Insurance Institute for Highway Safety provided additional funding through investigator initiated grants and contracts to the Pacific Institute for Research and Evaluation, NHTSA's contractor for the 2013–2014 NRS.

[2] .08 g/210 L = grams per 210 liters of breath. The illegal limit in all States is .08.

[3] From 1973 to 2004, the States had BrAC limits that ranged from .08 to .15. After 2004, all States had BrAC limits of .08.

[4] Despite recent changes in the legal status of marijuana in some States, for simplicity and to allow inter-survey comparisons, this drug remained included within the "illegal" category in the 2013– 2014 NRS.

[5] "Any Illegal Drug" includes drivers who tested positive for one or more illegal drugs, whether or not they also tested positive for medications.

[6] "Only Medications" includes drivers who tested positive for one or more medications, but did not test positive for illegal drugs.

In: Drug-Impaired Driving
Editor: Tobias H. Erickson
ISBN: 978-1-63482-871-0

Chapter 3

DRUG-IMPAIRED DRIVING: UNDERSTANDING THE PROBLEM AND WAYS TO REDUCE IT*

R. Compton, M. Vegega and D. Smither

ABSTRACT

This report was prepared in accordance with Section 2013 of the Safe, Accountable, Flexible, Efficient Transportation Equity Act: A Legacy for Users (SAFETEA-LU). The report summarizes a series of studies undertaken by the National Highway Traffic Safety Administration to acquire the information needed to address the general problem of drug-impaired driving.

The report describes the research conducted on prevention, detection, and prosecution of driving under the influence of drugs; issues associated with determining what drugs impair driving; difficulties in relating blood levels of drugs and impairment; lack of information about what drugs are frequently used by drivers and what drugs elevate crash risk; problems in obtaining representative data about current enforcement, prosecution, and adjudication of drug-impaired driving; training for law enforcement officers in recognizing drug-impaired drivers; review of drug-impaired driving laws; and what is known about the role of drugs as causal factors in traffic crashes. It highlights the need for further research and concludes

* This is an edited, reformatted and augmented version of a report to Congress, DOT HS 811 268, issued by the National Highway Traffic Safety Administration, December 2009.

with recommendations to better address the problem of drug-impaired driving.

Keywords: Drug-impaired driving, drugged driving, drugs and driving, DUID

INTRODUCTION

Section 2013 of the Safe, Accountable, Flexible, Efficient Transportation Equity Act: A Legacy for Users (SAFETEA-LU), enacted on August 10, 2005, directs the Secretary of Transportation to advise and coordinate with other Federal agencies on how to address the problem of driving under the influence of an illegal drug; to conduct research on the prevention, detection, and prosecution of driving under the influence of an illegal drug; and to submit to Congress a report on the problem of drug-impaired driving.

> *SEC. 2013. DRUG-IMPAIRED DRIVING ENFORCEMENT*
>
> (a) ILLICIT DRUG.—In this section, the term "illicit drug" includes substances listed in schedules I through V of section 112(e) of the Controlled Substances Act (21 U.S.C. 812) not obtained by a legal and valid prescription.
>
> (b) DUTIES. — The Secretary shall—
>
> 1. advise and coordinate with other Federal agencies on how to address the problem of driving under the influence of an illegal drug; and
> 2. conduct research on the prevention, detection, and prosecution of driving under the influence of an illegal drug.
>
> (c) REPORT.—
>
> 1. IN GENERAL. — Not later than 18 months after the date of enactment of this Act, the Secretary, in cooperation with the National Institutes of Health, shall submit to Congress a report on the problem of drug-impaired driving.
> 2. CONTENTS. — The report shall include, at a minimum, the following:
>   (A) An assessment of methodologies and technologies for measuring driver impairment resulting from use of the most common illicit drugs (including the use of such drugs in combination with alcohol).
>   (B) Effective and efficient methods for training law enforcement personnel, including drug recognition experts, to detect or measure the level of impairment of a driver who

is under the influence of an illicit drug by the use of technology or otherwise.

(C) A description of the role of drugs as causal factor in traffic crashes and the extent of the problem of drug impaired driving.

(D) A description and assessment of current State and Federal laws relating to drug-impaired driving.

(E) Recommendations for addressing the problem of drug-impaired driving, including recommendations on levels of impairment.

(F) Recommendations for developing a model statute relating to drug-impaired driving.

(d) MODEL STATUTE.—

1. IN GENERAL.—The Secretary shall develop a model statute for States relating to drug-impaired driving.
2. CONTENTS. — Based on recommendations and findings contained in the report submitted under subsection (c), the model statute may include—

(A) threshold levels of impairment for illicit drugs;

(B) practicable methods for detecting the presence of illicit drugs; and

(C) penalties for drug impaired driving.

(3) DATE. — The model statute shall be provided to States not later than 1 year after date of submission of the report under subsection (c).

(e) RESEARCH AND DEVELOPMENT. — Section 403(b) of title 23, United States Code, is amended by adding at the end the following:

5. Technology to detect drug use and enable States to efficiently process toxicology evidence.
6. Research on the effects of illicit drugs and the compound effects of alcohol and illicit drugs on impairment.".

(f) FUNDING. — Out of amounts made available to carry out section 403 of title 23, United States Code, for each of fiscal years 2006 through 2009, the Secretary shall make available $1,200,000 for such fiscal year to carry out this section.

This report documents the progress and the available results of the research conducted on the problem of drug-impaired driving, and recommends further steps for addressing the problem.

BACKGROUND

Drug-impaired driving is a complex problem due to the large number of substances with the potential to impair driving and increase crash risk, the variations in the ways different drugs can impair driving, the lack of basic information about many potentially impairing drugs, and the differences in the ways that drugs can affect the body and behavior. Other critical factors include the poorly understood pharmacokinetics and pharmacodynamics of many psychoactive drugs, in addition to the problems presented by individual differences, sensitivity, and tolerance, and the myriad of ways that various substances interact. A discussion of some of these issues is useful to appreciate the difficulties that must be overcome in addressing the drug-impaired driving problem.

Since the effects of alcohol on driving performance are relatively well understood, it is useful to review and contrast what is known about alcohol with what is known and not known about other drugs. Ethyl alcohol is a simple molecule that is readily and fairly rapidly absorbed into the body, typically through the stomach and large intestine. Alcohol passes easily through the blood-brain barrier. It is distributed by the circulatory system throughout the body and is metabolized primarily in the liver.

The processes of absorption, distribution, and metabolism of alcohol occur at the same time. The concentration of alcohol in the body can be measured in the blood (also in the breath and in other bodily substances) and a single dose will result in a rapid increase in blood concentration, reaching a peak, and then diminishing over a period of hours. Repeated dosing will raise the peak blood alcohol concentration (BAC) and prolong the time elevated levels are present in the body. The time course during which the effects of alcohol on the body and behavior can be measured parallels the time course during which BAC is elevated in the body. There is a close relationship between BAC level and impairment. Some effects are detectable at very low BACs (e.g., .02 grams per deciliter, or g/dL) and as BAC rises, the types and severity of impairment increase.

Unfortunately, the behavioral effects of other drugs are not as well understood as the behavioral effects of alcohol. Certain generalizations can be made: high doses generally have a larger effect than small doses; well-learned tasks are less affected than novel tasks; and certain variables, such as prior exposure to a drug, can either reduce or accentuate expected effects, depending on circumstances. The ability to predict an individual's performance at a specific dosage of drugs other than alcohol is limited.

Most psychoactive drugs are chemically complex molecules whose absorption, action, and elimination from the body are difficult to predict. Further, there are considerable differences between individuals with regard to the rates with which these processes occur. Alcohol, in comparison, is more predictable. A strong relationship between BAC level and impairment has been established, as has the correlation between BAC level and crash risk.

Factors that make similar prediction difficult for most other psychoactive drugs include:

- The large number of different drugs that would need to be tested (extensive testing of alcohol has been undertaken over many decades; whereas relatively little similar testing has occurred for most other drugs);
- Poor correlation between the effects on psychomotor, behavioral, and/or executive functions, and blood or plasma levels (peak psychomotor, behavioral, and executive function effects do not necessarily correspond to peak blood levels; detectable blood levels may persist beyond the impairing effects or the impairing effects may be measurable when the drug cannot be detected in the blood);
- Sensitivity and tolerance (accentuation and diminution of the impairing effects with repeated exposure);
- Individual differences in absorption, distribution, action, and metabolism (some individuals will show evidence of impairment at drug concentrations that are not associated with impairment in others; wide ranges of drug concentrations in different individuals have been associated with equivalent levels of impairment);
- Accumulation (blood levels of some drugs or their metabolites may accumulate with repeated administrations if the time-course of elimination is insufficient); and
- Acute versus chronic administration (it is not unusual to observe much larger impairment during initial administrations of drugs than is observed when the drug is administered over a long period of time).

The result of these factors is that, at the current time, specific drug concentration levels cannot be reliably equated with effects on driver performance.

REPORT OVERVIEW

In response to the direction provided by the Congress to the Secretary of Transportation, the National Highway Traffic Safety Administration undertook a series of studies to address issues raised in Section 2013 of SAFETEA-LU. These studies were designed to acquire information necessary to address the general problem of drug-impaired driving and the specific issues requested.

This report follows the order of the issues raised in Section 2013. While that section specifically mentions illegal drugs, many prescription drugs and some over-the-counter medications have similar potential to impair driving. Consequently, some of the research covers these drug types as well.

ADVISE AND COORDINATE WITH OTHER FEDERAL AGENCIES

The NHTSA has established a working group on driving under the influence of drugs with representatives from the National Institute on Drug Abuse, the National Institute on Alcoholism and Alcohol Abuse, the Substance Abuse and Mental Health Services Administration, the National Transportation Safety Board, and the National Center for Injury Prevention and Control, Centers for Disease Control and Prevention. This working group meets on an ad hoc basis and has discussed the problem of drug-impaired driving and ways to address the problem.

The working group assisted in the planning and conducting of two expert panel meetings to discuss the feasibility of establishing a methodology for identifying drugs that impair driving.

The working group helped ensure that relevant disciplines and expertise were represented on the expert panel and suggested leading experts in these fields. Members of the working group were also invited to participate in a discussion on the methodology for conducting a case-control study on drug-impaired driving.

Research on the Prevention, Detection, and Prosecution of Driving Under the Influence of Drugs (DUID)

The NHTSA has conducted research on drug-impaired driving for several decades. The agency periodically updates the literature on this topic through publication of state-of-the-knowledge reports on driving under the influence of drugs (DUID), the latest being issued in 2003 (Jones, Shinar, & Walsh, 2003). This research has taken the form of laboratory studies (Bigelow, Bickel, Liebson, & Nowowieski, 1985), driving simulator studies (Friedel et al., 1990, 1991; Moskowitz, & Wilkinson, 2004; Moskowitz, Ziedman, & Sharma, 1976), on-the-road studies of the effects of selected drugs on driving-related skills (Riedel, Quasten, Hausen, & O'Hanlon, 1988; Robbe & O'Hanlon, 1993, 1999), and literature reviews of selected research on drugs and driving (Dobbs, 2005; Moskowitz & Wilkinson, 2004; Robbe & O'Hanlon, 1993). Research has also been conducted into methods to aid law enforcement to recognize drug-impaired drivers (Bigelow et al., 1985; Compton, 1986, 1988; Compton, Preusser, Ulmer, & Preusser, 1997; Preusser, Ulmer, & Preusser, 1992; Shinar & Compton, 2002); the development of training courses for judges and prosecutors (National Highway Traffic Safety Administration [NHTSA], 2007b), and research into the accuracy of drug testing technology for law enforcement use (Crouch, Walsh, Cangianelli, & Quintela, 2008; Hersch, Crouch, & Cook, 2000; Walsh & Cangianelli, 2009). The NHTSA has also developed educational material for consumers on the dangers of using certain drugs and driving (NHTSA, 2004) and information for physicians on the potentially impairing effects of medications (Loccoco & Tyree, 2007; Wang, Kosinski, Schwartzberg, & Shanklin, 2003).

Recent research on these topics includes assembling a panel of experts to examine a variety of issues associated with the prosecution of drug-impaired drivers and the quality of supporting toxicology evidence (Logan, 2007). The NHTSA also funded the development of Drug Fact Sheets for the use of toxicologists and prosecutors, which contain information on the effects of a variety of frequently used substances that impair driving ability (Couper & Logan, 2004).

To better understand the current situation regarding drug-impaired driving enforcement, the NHTSA recently conducted a study to collect information on the enforcement, prosecution, and adjudication of drug-impaired driving in the States (Moulden, Cangianelli, Walsh, & Atkins, 2009). Also, the NHTSA conducted a research study to examine whether the adoption of drug per se laws produced a noticeable difference in the prosecution and conviction of drug-impaired driving (Lacey, Brainard, & Snitow, 2009). Fifteen States have enacted some version of drug per se statutes for selected illegal drugs (controlled substances). These laws make it illegal to drive with any amount of these drugs in the body. Some States set threshold levels above which the driver is presumed to be positive for the presence of the drug. These types of laws do not make specific reference to driver impairment as a result of drug use.

A further complication for understanding drug-impaired driving is the use of multiple potentially impairing substances. It is not uncommon for drivers to take two or three potentially impairing drugs at the same time. Drivers frequently combine use of drugs with alcohol. While many individual substances taken by themselves, at normal doses, may not impair driving sufficiently to raise crash risk, when taken together the effects may be synergistic and produce an increased risk of crash involvement. Limited research on the combined effects of substances has shown this to be the case. The NHTSA has recently conducted a number of studies designed to explore the potential risk of multiple medication use by drivers (LeRoy & Morse, 2008; Lococo & Staplin, 2006; Staplin, Lococo, Gish, & Martell, 2008).

MEASURING DRIVER IMPAIRMENT

Congress requested that an assessment of methodologies and technologies for measuring driver impairment resulting from use of the most common illicit drugs (including the use of such drugs in combination with alcohol) be conducted. The measurement of driver impairment is challenging since driver performance is a product of manual, cognitive, and perceptive skills and the range of performance reflected in the normal driver population is large.

Current knowledge about the effects of drugs other than alcohol is insufficient to allow the identification of dosage limits that are related to elevated crash risk. However, it is likely that better methods and technology to detect drug use by drivers would greatly facilitate the enforcement, prosecution, and adjudication of existing drug-impaired-driving laws. With this in mind, the NHTSA conducted a study to look at current methods and technologies to detect drug use by drivers (Walden & the Texas Transportation Institute, 2008).

The Impaired-Driving-Detection Process

The detection of driver drug impairment typically takes place as a result of a law enforcement officer observing inappropriate driving behavior. The officer will stop the vehicle and engage the driver in conversation while the driver is inside the vehicle. The officer at this time may form a suspicion that the driver is impaired. This suspicion can be based on observations of driving behavior, the appearance of the driver, the behavior of the driver, and any statements the driver has made about alcohol or drug use. If the officer suspects that the driver is impaired, the officer will request that the driver exit the vehicle, and the officer will proceed to conduct pre-arrest screening tests. This phase can include the use of the Standardized Field Sobriety Tests (SFSTs) that helps the officer determine whether the driver is impaired by alcohol and if the driver's BAC is likely to be above the legal limit.

Based on this information, the officer may place the driver under arrest for suspicion of impaired driving. At this point, the officer will request a BAC sample, typically a breath sample, but a blood or urine sample could be requested in lieu of breath. The officer may also take the offender to a booking location where a sample (of blood, breath, or urine) will be requested, or, in many instances, the officer may obtain a sample at the roadside in the patrol vehicle or in a mobile testing van or similar setting, if an evidential breath test device is available.

Since most driver impairment is from alcohol, an officer will typically begin by testing this possibility. Only when the BAC test results are incompatible with the observed impairment would an officer consider drugs other than alcohol (unless the driver exhibits signs and symptoms not indicative of alcohol use). Typically, if the suspect is found to be under the influence of alcohol, especially when the BAC is at or above the legal limit, the investigation stops, even if the officer has reason to suspect use of other drugs are contributing to the suspect's impairment.

There are several disincentives for investigating potential impairment due to drugs other than alcohol when BAC evidence clearly shows an illegal alcohol level. Generally, the alcohol charge meets the burden of proof, and State laws typically do not have additional penalties for multiple substance impairment.

However, if impairment is observed and BAC tests are negative, officers can seek additional evidence to support a drug-impaired driving charge. In jurisdictions that participate in the Drug Evaluation and Classification (DEC) Program, the arresting officer may request an evaluation by a Drug

Recognition Expert (DRE). This program, originally developed by the Los Angeles Police Department in the 1970s, trains officers to recognize the signs and symptoms of drug use as an aid to investigating suspected drug-impaired-driving cases. The DRE performs a drug influence evaluation on the suspected impaired driver in order to determine whether the observed impairment is likely to be due to drug use (and if so, what specific type of drugs) or whether the observed impairment is due to neurological conditions, illness, or disease. The DRE, or arresting officer in cases where no DRE is available, gathers a biological sample (blood or urine) to be analyzed by a toxicology lab to confirm the suspect had used a drug or drugs. Currently, there are about 6,000 DREs in the 46 States that participate in the DEC program.

Laboratory Testing

Because conviction for drug-impaired driving may depend on evidence of drug use through laboratory testing, the accuracy and reliability of the toxicology results is important. Unfortunately, there are no national standards for conducting these types of toxicology tests and considerable variation exists among laboratories in terms of equipment, procedures, and training of personnel conducting the tests.

In 2004, the NHTSA held an expert panel meeting with toxicologists, DREs, and prosecutors to discuss and identify potential issues associated with conducting toxicology tests for impaired-driving cases and to identify ways to improve the process (Logan, 2007). The meeting resulted in a report that described three steps to improve toxicology testing in impaired-driving cases: (1) survey labs about current practices; (2) establish a Web site with current information on alcohol, drugs, and impairment and toxicological resources; and (3) develop recommendations to standardize methods used in laboratories supporting the DEC programs. Thus far, three surveys tracking current and needed resources have been conducted, the recommendations have been published, and the Web site will soon be operational (Farrell, Kerrigan, & Logan, 2007).

Specimen Collection

To determine whether a suspected impaired driver has actually used a drug requires evidence that it is present in a biological specimen. Typically, urine or blood specimens are taken for this purpose and then sent to a laboratory for analysis. There may be a delay of days, weeks, or months before the results are known. Thus, an officer will not know the test results prior to the time the suspect is charged. Different biological specimens have advantages and disadvantages, depending on the purpose of the testing. Biological specimens for drug testing include:

- *Oral Fluid Testing* — The collection of oral fluid is minimally invasive and effective in detecting many types of drugs. The technology to rapidly, accurately, and reliably collect oral fluid at the point of arrest is quickly evolving. Devices that collect oral fluid for laboratory testing appear to be a reliable means of testing for recent drug use. Some companies market self-contained test kits that can be used by law enforcement; however, these point-of-arrest screening devices have not been proven to be accurate and reliable.
- *Sweat Testing* — The collection of sweat over time can produce a cumulative record of prior drug use. However, a positive sweat test result cannot be regarded as evidence of impairment at the time of an arrest or crash. Sweat testing has no advantages over oral fluid testing and is susceptible to contamination.
- *Hair Testing* — Although it is possible to test samples of hair for drug usage, the results are of limited utility for drug-impaired-driving cases. Positive hair test results cannot be used to demonstrate drug use at the time of driving. In addition, variations in hair growth and the addition of substances to the hair, such as coloring products, make it difficult to extrapolate when drug usage occurred and may also affect the results.
- *Urine Testing* — The drug testing methodology for urinalysis is well established. Drugs and drug metabolites are detectable in urine for several days (sometimes weeks) after the drug has been used. As a result, unless extremely high levels of a drug or metabolite are found, which would indicate recent use, urine test results generally cannot prove that a driver was under the influence of the drug at the time of arrest or testing.
- *Blood Testing* — Blood testing is considered the "gold standard" for testing for the presence of drugs in impaired driving cases. However, as described in the background section to this report, currently there is limited ability to relate the amount of a drug or metabolite in blood to

the presence and amount of impairment. Collecting a blood sample is an invasive procedure requiring a nurse or licensed phlebotomist.

Summary

The development of a method of measuring driver impairment due to the use of drugs would greatly enhance the ability of law enforcement to investigate suspected drug-impaired driving cases. However, there is currently no accurate and reliable way to measure the level or degree of driving impairment associated with the use of drugs.

DUID Law Enforcement and Adjudication

In order to understand the current status of DUID enforcement and prosecution in the United States, the NHTSA conducted a study to collect nationally representative data regarding the number of drivers arrested, prosecuted, and convicted of DUID in all 50 States. The study was also designed to compare States with and without the DEC program to determine whether the presence of Drug Recognition Experts affect the DUID arrest rate and to compare States with and without drug per se laws to determine whether these laws were associated with higher conviction rates (Moulden et al., 2009).

A lack of law enforcement, prosecution, and adjudication records posed a major challenge to the successful conduct of this research. While considerable effort was made to obtain the necessary arrest and disposition records for Driving While Intoxicated (DWI) by alcohol and DUID, this was not entirely successful. Chief among the difficulties were: the lack of statewide record systems for either arrest or disposition data and the inability to distinguish between DWI and DUID offenses. In those jurisdictions where samples of DUID arrest data could be obtained, the number of DUID arrests comprised a relatively small percentage of all impaired driving arrests, ranging from 2% to 16%. The State with the highest DUID arrest rate of 16%, Mississippi, has neither a DEC program nor a drug per se law. However, the lack of complete data does not allow conclusions to be drawn about the contribution of either the DEC program or the drug per se statute to enforcing drug-impaired driving.

It is likely that the lack of incentives for investigating drug impairment when alcohol is detected at BACs above .08 g/dL has led to fewer impaired drivers being arrested and prosecuted for drug-impaired driving than were encountered by law enforcement.

Methods for Training Law Enforcement Personnel

Training on drug-impaired driving is available to law enforcement officers in three increasingly detailed levels. Officers at the highest level of training are capable of making determinations about which drug category (or categories) may be contributing to a driver's inability to operate a vehicle. Depending on the individual State requirements, officers may or may not receive training in DUID prior to completing their basic training requirements.

To improve consistency in training, the NHTSA developed an 8-hour course, *Drugs That Impair Driving,* which can be used in conjunction with the SFST training. The NHTSA considers SFST training the foundation for all impaired driving detection training. The *Drugs That Impair Driving* course was developed to provide a general description of drugs, signs that may indicate drug use, and medical conditions that show signs similar to drug use. The course was also developed to acquaint officers with the most common types of drugs that impair driving.

A second level course, the 16-hour *Advanced Roadside Impaired Driving Enforcement Program*, is designed to give officers the ability to apply information they have learned about DUID to make effective arrests based on probable cause that provides the necessary evidence for prosecution. In order to accomplish this goal, the program seeks to increase the officer's overall knowledge of the general manifestations of alcohol and drug impairment and to increase their ability to recognize these indicators in the drivers they encounter during their enforcement duties. If these drivers are suspected to be impaired, then officers will be better informed in the arrest decision.

The highest level of training comes in the form of the DEC program (NHTSA, 2007a). In the early 1980s the NHTSA developed the DEC program based on the Los Angeles Police Department's DRE program. The DEC program trains officers to identify the signs and symptoms of drug use that could be used to determine whether a suspected impaired driver was impaired by drugs and to rule out other possible causes such as neurological deficits, diseases, and illness. The procedure was designed to aid the officer in determining what specific type of drug was the likely cause of the observed impairment. The program was intended to help develop evidence of impairment and guide the analyses of biological specimens when looking for the presence of drugs other than alcohol in impaired drivers. The DEC training requires 9 days in the classroom and additional days of field certification testing. The program is designed to provide a limited number of DREs in a jurisdiction. It is not designed for the routine patrol officer.

The Role of Drugs in Causing Traffic Crashes and the Extent of the Problem of Drug-Impaired Driving

The scope and magnitude of the drug-impaired driving problem in this country cannot be clearly specified at this time. However, a number of factors suggest that a problem exists, including the widespread use of drugs; the number of controlled substances, psychoactive prescription drugs, and over-the-counter medications that have the potential to impair driving; and specific studies indicating that many crash-involved drivers have used these drugs.

A better understanding of the drug-impaired-driving problem will require that several necessary types of information be obtained. These include:

- Which drugs impair driving ability;
- What drug dose levels are associated with impaired driving;
- How frequently drugs that impair driving are being used by drivers; and
- Which drugs are associated with higher crash rates.

As noted previously, it is important to know which drugs and dosage levels impair driving-related skills. This is a large undertaking, given the number of drugs with the potential to impair driving. Some laboratory research has been conducted on a number of high-priority drugs that measure the effects of drug usage on driving-related skills (e.g., divided attention, visual tracking, reaction time to sudden events). While the necessary connection to actual driving performance has not been established, laboratory tests have been useful to separate potentially hazardous drugs from those that do not produce performance impairment (such as non-narcotic analgesics like aspirin and ibuprofen). Thus, laboratory data can be used to focus attention on the drugs most likely to be highway safety problems.

Once it has been shown that a drug produces driving-related performance impairment in the laboratory, it becomes important to know the frequency with which people drive after having consumed that drug, and the extent to which crash risk is increased. Determining the frequency with which people drive after having consumed drugs may be approached in several different ways. These include questionnaires to obtain self-reported data on drug use and driving and roadside surveys of a representative sample of drivers that involve the collection and analysis of body fluids (e.g., blood or saliva) for the presence and amount of drugs.

Self-report data can be affected by biases. Respondents can be subject to pressure to give socially responsible answers, distrust that responses will be anonymous, or give misleading or inaccurate information. A more accurate determination of drug use by drivers can be made by collecting and analyzing body fluids.

Estimating the crash risk caused by drug use is important to verify that drugs that are known to impair performance on laboratory tasks have a measurable effect on actual crash risk.

One method to estimate the crash risk associated with drug use involves a comparison of the frequency of drug use by crash- and non-crash-involved drivers. Finding that the incidence of drug use in crash-involved drivers is higher than in non-crash involved drivers strongly suggests that the drugs may have contributed to the occurrence of the crashes. If use of a drug is unrelated to crash risk, there should be no difference in the number of crash-involved and non-crashinvolved drivers using the drug.

Knowing only the frequency with which crash-involved drivers use drugs does not directly indicate the crash risk of drug use, since drug use rates for crash-involved drivers may simply reflect the drug use pattern in the general driving public. For example, finding a certain use rate of nicotine or caffeine in crash-involved drivers may simply reflect the use pattern for these drugs in the general driving population and does not imply they played a role in the occurrence of the crashes. Only finding that a drug was overrepresented in crash-involved drivers in comparison to non-crash-involved drivers would indicate that drug use is associated with crash risk.

The NHTSA has recently undertaken new research to identify drugs that may affect driving and to assess their association with crash risk.

Expert Panel to Develop a Protocol for Determining Whether a Drug Is Likely to Impair Driving

Better information about which drugs have the potential to impair driving would be helpful in several respects. Not only would it focus further research attention on relevant drugs, it would also assist physicians and pharmacists in providing patient warnings and education. In addition, it would allow consumers to be educated on the potential dangers of combining use of specific drugs and driving. In order to facilitate research to identify drugs with the potential to impair driving, the NHTSA recently convened an expert panel to determine the feasibility of developing a method or protocol that would be generally accepted for establishing whether a particular drug (over-the-counter, prescription, or illegal) is likely to impair driving, and if so, how such a protocol would be established. The panel was composed of behavioral scientists, epidemiologists, toxicologists and traffic safety professionals to provide a broad based perspective on the issue.

The panel determined that while it is not currently possible to produce a list of drugs that impair driving, it is feasible to determine the likely effects of drugs on driving and laid out a general process to be followed to evaluate any specific drug for the potential likelihood to impair driving. A tiered approach to assessing drugs was suggested that would start with an evaluation of the basic pharmacological data on a drug to determine whether it was psychoactive or otherwise likely to produce effects that might impair driving.

The next step would be to test the drug for its effects on critical driving-related skills or functions. These would take the form of testing for impairment on such functions as simple and complex reaction time, alertness/arousal, sensory/perceptual functioning, attention/information processing demand, and executive functions (e.g., planning, decision-making, monitoring/vigilance). The panel proposed a process to develop and validate a test battery for this purpose and specified criteria that acceptable tests would have to meet that include accuracy, reliability, sensitivity, and validity.

The next level of testing would involve the use of driving simulators and over-the-road testing employing approaches such as the Standardized Driving Test. Finally, additional data could be obtained by using instrumented vehicles. The panel recognized that each of these levels of assessment provides incremental evidence as to the impairing nature of drugs and can be used together to reach a more complete understanding of the risks associated with a particular drug. A final level of evidence would be an indication that the drug is overrepresented in crashes.

A summary report on the expert panel's recommended approach to determining whether a drug is likely to impair driving is expected in 2010.

2007 National Roadside Survey of Alcohol and Drug Use by Drivers

The NHTSA recently conducted the first nationally representative roadside survey of alcohol and drug use by drivers. The 2007 National Roadside Survey (NRS) involved random stops of drivers at 300 locations across the contiguous United States. Data were primarily collected on weekend nights (10 p.m. to midnight on Fridays and Saturdays and 1 a.m. to 3 a.m. on Saturdays and Sundays), but also included weekday daytime data collection (Fridays 9:30 a.m. to 11:30 a.m. or 1:30 p.m. to 3:30 p.m.).

Participation in the survey was voluntary and anonymous. Whereas prior alcohol roadside surveys excluded commercial vehicles and motorcycles, the 2007 NRS included motorcycles. Almost 11,000 eligible drivers entered the survey sites. Biological measures included breath-alcohol measurements on 9,413 drivers (86%), oral fluid samples from 7,719 drivers (71%), and blood samples from 3,276 nighttime drivers (39%). The study will identify use of a variety of drugs including over-the-counter medications, prescription, and illegal drugs. Drug categories included in the tests are stimulants, sedatives, antidepressants, marijuana, and narcotic analgesics. The study is examining drug use by driver age, gender, income, employment status, education, vehicle type, alcohol and drug abuse syndromes, and other socio-demographic variables.

The results of this study are expected to be released soon. The 2007 NRS will, for the first time, provide national prevalence rates for drug use by drivers. As discussed earlier in this report, drug use by drivers does not necessarily imply impairment. For many drug types, drug presence can be detected long after any impairment that might affect driving has passed. For example, traces of marijuana can be detected in blood samples several weeks after ingestion.

Crash Risk of Driving After Using Drugs

The NHTSA has another large-scale study under way to estimate the crash risk of drug use by drivers. This case–control study will compare the incidence of drug use by crash-involved drivers to similarly exposed non-crash-involved drivers. Data collection started in 2009 and will extend for at least one year in a large metropolitan area. A random sample of at least 2,500 crashes reported to the police will be included, along with 5,000 control subjects stopped at the same locations, same day of week, time of day, and direction of travel, one week later.

This study will allow for an estimation of the risk of crash involvement associated with drug use. Due to the complexity, difficulty, and expense of conducting this type of research, it is likely that only a few drugs other than alcohol will be detected with sufficient frequency to allow for crash risk estimation. Data collection and analysis will take approximately 2 years to complete.

Current State Laws Relating to Drug-Impaired Driving

The NHTSA commissioned a review of each State statute regarding drug-impaired driving as of December 2008 (Walsh, 2009). The DUID statutes are generally found in the State Transportation Code or Title, or Motor Vehicle Code or Title. In only two States (Idaho and Texas) can the State's DUID statutes be found in the penal or criminal codes.

There is a high degree of variability across the States in the way they approach drug-impaired driving. Current laws in many States contain provisions making it difficult to identify, prosecute, or convict drug-impaired drivers.

State laws commonly identify drug-impaired driving in one of the following three ways:

1) The presence of drugs renders a driver incapable of driving safely;
2) The driver is under the influence or affected by an intoxicating drug; or
3) A per se statue that makes it a criminal offense for a driver to have a drug or metabolite in his/her body while operating a motor vehicle.

The first two types of laws are most prevalent. In such cases a State must prove that the drug "caused" the impaired driving (i.e., a prosecutor must show a connection between drug ingestion and the incapacity or impairment of the driver). Fifteen States have drug per se statutes (which are actually zero tolerance statutes since they typically make it illegal to drive with any amount of specified illegal drugs in the driver's body). In seven States (Arizona, Delaware, Georgia, Indiana, Minnesota, Pennsylvania and Utah) it is illegal to have any amount of a drug or its metabolite in the body while operating a motor vehicle (note: the Minnesota law exempts marijuana). In five States (Illinois, Iowa, Michigan, Rhode Island and Wisconsin) it is illegal to have any amount of a prohibited drug in the body while operating a motor vehicle. Three States (Nevada, Ohio and Virginia) it is illegal to have specific amounts of specified prohibited substances in the body while operating a motor vehicle. Two States (North Carolina and South Dakota) make it illegal for people under age 21 to drive with any amount of a prohibited drug or substance in their bodies. Five States (California, Colorado, Idaho, Kansas and West Virginia) make it illegal for any drug addict or habitual user of drugs to drive a vehicle.

Only two States (Hawaii and New York) have DUID statutes separate from their alcohol DUI laws. In all other States, a driver violates a DUI statute if the driver drives under the influence of alcohol, drugs, or a combination of alcohol and drugs. The violation is the same, as are the penalties. The one exception is the State of Washington, in which there are different penalties for drug use only, as opposed to alcohol use or a combination of alcohol and drug use.

Twenty States (Alabama, Arizona, Arkansas, Delaware, Georgia, Idaho, Illinois, Kansas, Kentucky, Montana, North Carolina, Oklahoma, Pennsylvania, Rhode Island, South Dakota, Tennessee, Texas, Vermont, Washington, and West Virginia) and Puerto Rico specifically disallow legal entitlement to use the drug as a defense to a DUID charge. Use of a drug pursuant to a valid prescription and/or according to directions is a defense to a DUID charge in several States.

All but five States (Alabama, Alaska, Massachusetts, New Jersey and West Virginia) extend their implied consent laws (i.e., to provide a specimen if requested by law enforcement) to DUID. However, both Alabama and Alaska make a provision for compulsory testing in cases involving serious injury or fatal crashes. Of the remaining 45 States (plus the District of Columbia and Puerto Rico) that extend their implied consent laws to drug-impaired driving, nine States (Arizona, Indiana, Louisiana, Maryland, Minnesota, Nebraska, New Mexico, Ohio and Rhode Island) provide criminal penalties for a refusal to take a test under the implied consent law. Twenty-eight States and the District of Columbia and Puerto Rico allow for a forced taking of a specimen over the objection of the driver, but this is generally in cases of a serious injury or fatal crash, and there is probable cause that the driver was under the influence of a drug.

Under implied consent provisions, most State laws stipulate the type of specimen that police officers are authorized to collect. Thirty-four States permit blood and/or urine; eight States allow for blood collection only; six States permit saliva; and eight States plus Puerto Rico permit "other bodily substances."

With respect to sanctions, some States have relatively light sentences for first offenders, while others are more severe in their handling of first offenders. Some States have made a second or third offense a felony, whereas in other States felony status is not reached until the fourth or subsequent offense. Penalties including fines and incarceration differ from State to State. Many States use community service, house arrest, electronic monitoring, work release, restitution, and assessment of cost and fees to supplement the court's ability to sanction offenders. Approximately 35 States provide for court-ordered substance abuse treatment and/or education for offenders. A growing number of States require participation in a program or treatment as a condition of probation or as a prerequisite to reinstatement of driving privileges.

Clearly, there is great variability among the States in how they approach driving under the influence of drugs. Having no separate offense for driving under the influence of drugs makes it difficult to distinguish between DUID and DWI-alcohol arrest and disposition. A recent attempt to investigate the effectiveness of drug per se laws was unable to draw conclusions due to the paucity of objective data and the inability of State data systems to distinguish between DUID and DWI-alcohol arrests and convictions (Lacey, Brainard, & Snitow, 2009). In addition, in cases where a driver shows evidence of impairment by multiple substances, the lack of difference in sanctions between drug-impaired and alcohol-impaired driving provides little incentive for criminal justice officials to pursue a drug-impaired driving charge in addition to an alcohol offense.

RECOMMENDATIONS FOR ADDRESSING THE PROBLEM OF DRUG-IMPAIRED DRIVING

This report has reviewed a variety of information pertaining to drug-impaired driving, including issues associated with determining which drugs impair driving, the difficulties that exist in relating blood levels of drugs to degree of impairment, the lack of information about which drugs are frequently used by drivers and which drugs elevate crash risk, the problems in obtaining representative data about current enforcement, prosecution, and adjudication of drug-impaired driving. The report also described three levels of training for law enforcement officers for recognizing drug-impaired drivers, reviews drug-impaired driving laws, and discusses what is known about the role of drugs as causal factors in traffic crashes.

The report highlights the need for further research and specifically points to the need for better data and information systems to allow continued progress in understanding and addressing the drug-impaired driving problem.

In particular, a lack of statewide arrest or disposition data distinguishing drug-impaired from alcohol-impaired driving arrests significantly impedes the States' ability to assess the extent of drug-impaired driving and evaluate the impact of countermeasures. Similarly, the lack of standardized and complete State record systems limits the NHTSA's ability to make clear inferences about the scope of the national drug-impaired-driving problem.

Better records would allow States to evaluate the impact of the DEC program on DUID arrest rates and convictions. Similarly, accurate and complete data about arrests and convictions for drug-impaired driving would allow documentation of the effects of drug per se statutes on arrest and convictions.

The NHTSA recommends the following data and record system improvements:

- States should develop record systems that distinguish among alcohol, drugs, or both for impaired driving cases. These records should be integrated into computerized data systems of law enforcement agencies, the court record systems, and motor vehicle records. One way to accomplish this would be to have separate offenses for driving impaired by alcohol and driving impaired by drugs.
- State records systems should document which drugs drug-impaired drivers are using. This information would be helpful for law enforcement, toxicologists, and prosecutors.
- Standard screening methodologies should be developed for drug testing laboratories to use in identifying drugs that impair driving. These methodologies should include standard analytic procedures and minimum detection thresholds. There also should be training requirements for the personnel operating these tests.

In addition to these data and record system needs, the NHTSA recommends the following change in State statutes:

- State statutes should be amended to provide separate and distinct sanctions for alcohol- and drug-impaired driving that could be applied individually or in combination to a single case. This would provide an incentive for law enforcement officers to pursue a possible drug-impaired driving charge even when a BAC equal to or above the limit of .08 g/dL has already been established.

Adoption of these recommendations would lead to a greater understanding of the drug-impaireddriving problem and ways to effectively reduce drug-impaired-driving crashes.

Recommendations for Developing a Model Statute Relating to Drug-Impaired Driving

The NHTSA, working with the National Traffic Law Center at the American Prosecutors Research Institute, National District Attorneys Association, has drafted a model drug-impaired driving law:

Model Drug-Impaired Driving Statute

Offenses —

A. It shall be unlawful for a person to drive or be in actual physical control of a vehicle in this State under any of the following circumstances:

1. While under the influence of any controlled substance, drug or any other substance which renders him or her incapable of safely driving; or
2. While under the influence of any combination of alcohol, controlled substance, drug or any other substance which renders him or her incapable of safely driving.

B. It is not a defense to a charge of a violation of subsection A, paragraphs 1 or 2 of this section if the person is or has been entitled to use the controlled substance, drug or other substance under the laws of this State.

Definitions —
The following definitions shall apply to this section:

(A) "Controlled substance," for the purposes of this section, shall have the meaning ascribed to it by [insert specific State reference under Uniform Controlled Substances Act].
(B) "Drug" shall include any substance, when taken into the human body, which can impair the ability of the person to operate a vehicle safely.

Official Remarks

The model statute does not contain any provisions for a per se (either specific level or zero-tolerance) prohibition because of the lack of a clear correlation between blood drug concentrations and impairment for many drugs.

It is strongly recommended that there be an enhanced or greater penalty for multiple (or poly-) drug use (including alcohol) compared to situations in which the driver is under the influence of only one substance. However, specific recommendations for sentencing have been excluded due to the variety of State-specific methodology and mechanisms for imposing sanctions (Logan, 2007).[1,2]

References

Bigelow, G. E., Bickel, W. E., Liebson, I. A, & Nowowieski, P. (1985). Identifying types of drug intoxication: Laboratory evaluation of a subject-examination procedure (DOT HS 806 753). Washington, DC: National Highway Traffic Safety Administration.

Compton, R. P. (1986). Field evaluation of the Los Angeles Police Department drug detection procedure (DOT HS 807 012). Washington, DC: National Highway Traffic Safety Administration.

Compton, R.P. (1988). Use of controlled substances and highway safety: A report to Congress (DOT HS 807 261). Washington, DC: National Highway Traffic Safety Administration.

Compton, R. P., Preusser, D. G., Ulmer, R. G., & Preusser, C. W. (1997). Impact of drug evaluation and classification on impaired driving enforcement. In the Proceedings of the 14th International Conference on Alcohol, Drugs and Traffic Safety, Annecy, France.

Couper, F. J., & Logan, B. K. (2004). Drugs and human performance fact sheets (DOT HS 809 725). Washington, DC: National Highway Traffic Safety Administration.

Crouch, D. J., Walsh, J. M., Cangianelli, L., & Quintela, O. (2008). Laboratory evaluation and field application of roadside oral fluid collectors and drug testing devices. Therapeutic Drug Monitor, 30, 188-195.

Dobbs, B. M. (2005). Medical conditions and driving: A review of the scientific literature (1960 –2000) (DOT HS 809 690). Washington, DC: National Highway Traffic Safety Administration.

Farrell, L. J., Kerrigan, S., & Logan, B. K. (2008). Recommendations for toxicological investigation of drug-impaired driving. *Journal of Forensic Sciences*, 52, 1214-1218.

Friedel, B., Joo, S., Reker, K., Kading, W., Klostermann, P., Saturnus, K. S., & Schneider, V. (1990). Test drives in the Daimler-Benz driving simulator with drivers under diazepam (DOT HS 807 569). Washington, DC: National Highway Traffic Safety Administration.

Friedel, B, Joo, S., Reker, K., Kading, W., Klostermann, P., Saturnus, K. S., & Schneider, V. (1991). Test drivers in the Daimler-Benz driving simulator with drivers under diphenhydramine (DOT HS 807 668). Washington, DC: National Highway Traffic Safety Administration.

Hersch, R. K., Crouch, D. J., & Cook, R. F. (2000). Field test of on-site drug detection devices. (DOT HS 809 192). Washington, DC: National Highway Traffic Safety Administration.

Jones, R. K., Shinar, D., & Walsh, J. M. (2003). State of knowledge of drug-impaired driving. (DOT HS 809 642). Washington, DC: National Highway Traffic Safety Administration.

Lacey, J., Brainard, K., & Snitow, S. (2009). Drug per se laws: A review of their use in States. Manuscript submitted for publication.

LeRoy, A. A., & Morse, M. L. (2008). Multiple medications and vehicle crashes: analysis of databases. (DOT HS 810 858). Washington, DC: National Highway Traffic Safety Administration.

Loccoco, K., & Tyree, R. (2007). Medication-related impaired driving (curriculum). (ACPE 254-999-07-036-H05-T). Walgreens Health Initiatives, Inc.

Loccoco, K. H., & Staplin, L. (2006). Polypharmacy and older drivers: Identifying strategies to study drug usage and driver functioning among older drivers (DOT HS 810 681). Washington, DC: National Highway Traffic Safety Administration.

Logan, B. K. (2007). Priorities and strategies for improving the investigation, use of toxicology results, and prosecution of drug-impaired driving cases: Findings and recommendations (DOT HS 810 708). Washington, DC: National Highway Traffic Safety Administration.

Moskowitz, H., & Wilkinson, C. J. (2004). Antihistamines and driving-related behavior: A review of the evidence for impairment. (DOT HS 809 714). Washington, DC: National Highway Traffic Safety Administration.

Moskowitz, H., Ziedman, K., & Sharma, S. (1976). Effect of marihuana and alcohol on visual search performance (DOT HS 802 052). Washington, DC: National Highway Traffic Safety Administration.

Moulden, J. V., Cangianelli, L. A., Walsh, J. M., & Atkins, R. (2009). Status of DUID enforcement and adjudication in DEC and non-DEC states. Manuscript submitted for publication.

National Highway Traffic Safety Administration. (2004, August). Driving when you are taking medication (DOT HS 809 777). Washington, DC: Author.

National Highway Traffic Safety Administration. (2007a). Drug evaluation and classification training: "The Drug Recognition Expert School" student manual. Washington, DC: Author.

National Highway Traffic Safety Administration. (2007b). Traffic safety resource prosecutors manual (DOT HS 810 706). Washington, DC: Author.

Preusser, D. F., Ulmer, R. G., Preusser, C. W., & Shinar, D. (1992). Evaluation of the impact of the drug evaluation and classification program on enforcement and adjudication (DOT HS 808 058). Washington, DC: National Highway Traffic Safety Administration.

Riedel, W. J., Quasten, R., Hausen, C., & O'Hanlon, J. F. (1988). A study comparing the hypnotic efficacies and residual effects on actual driving performance of midazolam 15 mg, triazolam 0.5 mg, temazepam 20 mg and placebo in shiftworkers on night duty (DOT HS EPX 018). Washington, DC: National Highway Traffic Safety Administration.

Robbe, H. W. J., & O'Hanlon, J. F. (1993). Marijuana and actual driving performance (DOT HS 808 078). Washington, DC: National Highway Traffic Safety Administration.

Robbe, H. W. J., & O'Hanlon, J. F. (1999). Marijuana, alcohol and actual driving performance (DOT HS 808 939). Washington, DC: National Highway Traffic Safety Administration.

Shinar, D., & Compton, R. P. (2002, August). Detecting and identifying drug impaired drivers based on observable signs and symptoms. In the Proceedings of the 16th International Conference on Alcohol, Drugs and Traffic Safety, Montreal, Canada.

Shinar, D., Schechtman, E., & Compton, R. P. (2000, May). Signs and symptoms predictive of drug impairment. In the Proceedings of the 15th International Conference on Alcohol, Drugs, & Traffic Safety, Stockholm, Sweden.

Staplin, L., Lococo, K. H., Gish, K. W., & Martell, C. (2008). A pilot study to test multiple medication usage and driving functioning (DOT HS 810 980). Washington, DC: National Highway Traffic Safety Administration.

The Walsh Group. (2002). The feasibility of per se drugged driving legislation consensus report 2002 (Robert Wood Johnson Foundation Substance Abuse Policy Research Program, Grant ID No. 040023). Princeton, NJ: Robert Wood Johnson Foundation.

Transportation Research Board. (2000, September). Transportation research e-circular: Issues and methods in the detection of alcohol and other drugs (Number E-C02). Washington, DC: Author.

Walden, M., & Texas Transportation Institute. (2008). Review and assessment of methods and technologies for detecting and testing drugs in drivers. Unpublished manuscript, National Highway Traffic Safety Administration, Washington, DC.

Walsh, J. M. (2009). A State-by-State analysis of laws dealing with driving under the influence of drugs (DOT HS 811 236). Washington, DC: National Highway Traffic Safety Administration.

Walsh, J. M., & Cangianelli, L. A. (2009). ROSITA II: Roadside testing and assessment—Results from US sites. Manuscript submitted for publication.

Wang, C. C., Kosinski, C. J., Schwartzberg, J. G., & Shanklin, A. V. (2003). Physician's guide to assessing and counseling older drivers (DOT HS 809 647). Washington, DC: National Highway Traffic Safety Administration.

End Notes

[1] See also, Transportation Research E-Circular: Issues and Methods in the Detection of Alcohol and Other Drugs (Number E-C020), September 2000.

[2] The Walsh Group. (2002). The feasibility of per se drugged driving legislation consensus report 2002 (Robert Wood Johnson Foundation Substance Abuse Policy Research Program, Grant ID No. 040023). Princeton, NJ: Robert Wood Johnson Foundation.

INDEX

A

access, 24, 26
accreditation, 37
adjustment, 56
adolescents, 12
adverse effects, 22, 37
advertisements, 29
advocacy, vii, 2, 6, 33, 34, 37
age, 36, 47, 51, 53, 56, 91, 93
agencies, vii, 1, 3, 5, 6, 7, 12, 13, 14, 21, 24, 25, 26, 29, 30, 31, 32, 33, 43, 76, 95
Alaska, 36, 93
alcohol use, vii, 10, 12, 21, 39, 40, 49, 54, 56, 57, 64, 66, 83, 93
alcohol-impaired driving, vii, 1, 3, 5, 7, 12, 13, 20, 22, 30, 31, 72, 94, 95
alertness, 8, 18, 90
amphetamines, 8, 11, 17, 27
antidepressants, 11, 17, 46, 65, 91
anxiety, 8, 15, 18
anxiety disorder, 8
appropriations, 37
arousal, 90
arrest(s), 2, 9, 12, 13, 14, 19, 22, 26, 83, 85, 86, 87, 94, 95
assessment, 10, 76, 77, 82, 90, 94, 100
attitudes, 3, 11, 30, 31
audit, 6, 35
authority, 35
awareness, 3, 20, 21, 29, 30, 31

B

BAC, 3, 7, 13, 16, 27, 30, 35, 43, 55, 78, 79, 83, 96
barbiturates, 11
behaviors, 3, 11, 30, 31, 36, 59
Belgium, 42
benefits, 31
bias, 40, 41, 56, 57
biological samples, 26, 36
blood, viii, 3, 7, 8, 9, 10, 16, 17, 19, 22, 27, 36, 37, 41, 42, 44, 52, 57, 65, 66, 68, 69, 71, 75, 78, 79, 83, 84, 85, 89, 91, 94, 97
blood pressure, 8
blood stream, 66
blood-brain barrier, 78
body fluid, 89
brain, 8, 66
breathing, 8

C

caffeine, 89
campaigns, 20, 25, 29, 30, 31
cannabinoids, 9, 17, 44, 65, 68
cannabis, 8, 15, 36
category a, 47, 48, 49
CDC, 3, 6, 7, 34

central nervous system, 16
certification, 14, 24, 88
challenges, vii, 1, 2, 5, 16, 19, 21, 23, 25, 31, 32, 33, 57, 58
chemical, 8, 17, 37
cities, 68
classes, 17, 44, 46, 47
classification, 98, 99
classroom, 23, 25, 88
cocaine, 8, 11, 15, 27
cognitive function, viii, 40
college students, 12, 36
collisions, 3, 20
combined effect, 82
commercial, 33, 53, 70, 91
community, 29, 94
community service, 94
complexity, 57, 92
compounds, 8, 19
conference, 33
Congress, vii, 1, 7, 37, 60, 75, 76, 80, 82, 98
consensus, 100, 101
consent, 36, 53, 93, 94
consumers, 81, 90
contamination, 85
controlled studies, 41, 57
controlled substances, 27, 82, 88, 98
Controlled Substances Act, 76, 97
conviction, 26, 82, 84, 86
cooperation, 43, 76
coordination, 24, 31
correlation, 70, 71, 79, 97
cost, 17, 23, 94
cough, 11, 36
cough suppressant, 11
counseling, 100
covering, 36, 42
CT, 59
current limit, 40
curriculum, 99

D

Daimler-Benz, 98
danger, 20
data collection, 15, 54, 57, 69, 91
database, 14, 24
deciliter, 78
deficit, 27
demographic factors, 56
Denmark, 42
Department of Commerce, 37
Department of Health and Human Services, 3, 4, 6, 34, 35
Department of Justice, 3, 7, 37
Department of Transportation, 61
depressants, 16
depression, 8
detectable, 16, 19, 26, 27, 35, 36, 66, 71, 78, 79, 85
detection, viii, 17, 25, 67, 75, 76, 83, 87, 95, 97, 98, 100
diphenhydramine, 98
diseases, 87
disorder, 27, 36
disposition, 86, 94, 95
distribution, 54, 71, 78, 79
District of Columbia, 7, 23, 36, 93
DOJ, 3, 7, 25, 37
donations, 37
dosage, 58, 78, 82, 88
dosing, 59, 78
DOT, 2, 32, 35, 39, 60, 61, 63, 72, 75, 97, 98, 99, 100
draft, 32
driving tasks, viii, 40
driving-related skills, viii, 39, 55, 81, 88, 90
drug abuse, 33, 91
drug addict, 93
drug courts, 26
drug metabolism, 8
drug testing, 2, 12, 15, 17, 19, 22, 25, 26, 30, 37, 81, 85, 95, 98
drugged-driving laws, vii, 2
drug-impaired driving, vii, viii, 1, 2, 3, 5, 6, 7, 9, 12, 13, 15, 19, 21, 22, 24, 25, 29, 30, 31, 32, 33, 34, 35, 39, 75, 76, 77, 78, 80, 81, 82, 83, 84, 86, 87, 88, 92, 93, 94, 95, 96, 98, 99
DWI, 86, 94

E

education, 3, 20, 21, 25, 30, 37, 90, 91, 94
e-mail, 26
emergency, 59
employment, 91
employment status, 91
enforcement, ix, 2, 12, 13, 14, 18, 20, 23, 24, 25, 29, 31, 34, 75, 81, 82, 86, 87, 95, 98, 99
equipment, 17, 19, 84
ethnicity, 47, 56
European Union (EU), 42
evidence, viii, 2, 3, 6, 13, 19, 21, 25, 26, 27, 31, 35, 39, 55, 57, 58, 66, 71, 77, 79, 81, 83, 84, 85, 87, 90, 94, 99
examinations, 23
executive function(s), 59, 71, 79, 90
expertise, 30, 80
exposure, 71, 78, 79

F

fatalities, vii, 1, 3, 5, 7, 20, 30, 31, 37
federal government, 7
financial, 57
financial resources, 57
Finland, 42
fluid, 8, 10, 11, 19, 22, 25, 27, 31, 36, 37, 41, 42, 44, 50, 52, 53, 54, 57, 65, 66, 68, 69, 85, 91, 98
Food and Drug Administration (FDA), 3, 6, 7, 17, 22, 34, 37
France, 98
funding, 7, 23, 25, 29, 35, 43, 73
funds, 7, 35, 73

G

GAO, vii, 1, 2, 5, 10, 13, 18, 28, 37
generalizability, 42, 57
Georgia, 93
grant programs, 7
grants, 23, 35, 73
growth, 85
guidance, 7, 22, 25, 33, 37

H

hair, 85
Hawaii, 22, 93
health, 12, 31, 36
heart rate, 8
heroin, 8, 27
HHS, vii, 1, 3, 4, 6, 7, 14, 22, 30, 32, 34, 36, 37
high school, 12, 36
House, 5
House of Representatives, 5
Housing and Urban Development, 4, 5, 32
human, 36, 52, 97, 98
human body, 97
human subjects, 52

I

ibuprofen, 88
ID, 100, 101
identification, 82
IIHS, viii, 63
illegal drug use, 36, 66
illegal substances, viii, 39
improvements, 3, 21, 23, 24, 68, 95
inattention, 59
incarceration, 94
incidence, 72, 89, 91
income, 91
individual differences, 78
individuals, 7, 16, 28, 58, 70, 71, 79
industry, 31
inferences, 95
information processing, 90
informed consent, 53
ingestion, 45, 66, 91, 92
injury(s), vii, 1, 3, 5, 7, 20, 30, 31, 37, 52, 57, 93
Insurance Institute for Highway Safety, viii, 6, 35, 63, 73

interaction effect, 49
interest groups, 34
interface, 24
intoxication, 97
Iowa, 93
irritability, 18
issues, viii, 7, 75, 78, 80, 81, 84, 94
Italy, 42

J

jurisdiction, 14, 42, 69, 88

L

labeling, 22
laboratory studies, 81
laboratory tests, 88
language barrier, 53
large intestine, 78
law enforcement, ix, 2, 6, 12, 14, 18, 19, 20, 21, 23, 24, 25, 26, 31, 69, 75, 76, 81, 83, 85, 86, 87, 93, 95, 96
laws, vii, ix, 2, 6, 7, 9, 16, 25, 26, 27, 28, 33, 34, 35, 37, 75, 77, 82, 83, 86, 92, 93, 94, 95, 97, 98, 100
laws and regulations, 33
lead, 59, 96
legislation, 7, 100, 101
light, 94
Lithuania, 42
liver, 78
longitudinal study, 36
Louisiana, 93

M

magnitude, 88
majority, 14, 69
marijuana, vii, viii, 2, 6, 7, 8, 9, 10, 11, 12, 14, 15, 16, 17, 18, 20, 22, 29, 30, 31, 34, 36, 39, 40, 41, 43, 44, 48, 57, 58, 66, 68, 73, 91, 93
marketing, 20
Maryland, 93
materials, 3, 29
measurement(s), 41, 44, 82, 91
media, 3, 29
medical, viii, 3, 6, 7, 28, 30, 31, 34, 39, 68, 87
medication(s), viii, 5, 8, 11, 15, 17, 20, 22, 27, 29, 30, 31, 33, 39, 46, 63, 68, 73, 80, 81, 82, 88, 91, 98, 99, 100
meta-analysis, 41
metabolism, 71, 78, 79
metabolites, 8, 9, 66, 71, 79, 85
metabolized, 16, 78
methodology, 6, 10, 11, 17, 36, 44, 52, 71, 80, 85, 97
Mexico, 93
Miami, 26
mission, 3, 29, 34
molecular structure, 17
molecules, 16, 70, 79
Montana, 93
morphine, 15
muscle relaxation, 8

N

narcolepsy, 27
narcotic, 44, 46, 48, 65, 88, 91
narcotic analgesics, 46, 48, 65, 88, 91
narcotics, 15
National Drug Control Strategy, 5
National Highway Traffic Safety Administration, vii, viii, 2, 4, 5, 10, 18, 34, 35, 39, 43, 59, 60, 61, 63, 64, 72, 73, 75, 80, 81, 97, 98, 99, 100
National Institutes of Health, 4, 6, 34, 35, 38, 76
National Survey, 4, 12, 35, 36
nervousness, 18
Netherlands, 42
NHTSA, vii, 1, 2, 3, 4, 5, 6, 7, 9, 10, 13, 15, 18, 20, 21, 22, 23, 24, 25, 26, 27, 29, 30, 31, 32, 34, 37, 40, 43, 53, 54, 55, 58, 63, 68, 72, 73, 80, 81, 82, 84, 86, 87, 89, 90, 91, 92, 95, 96

nicotine, 89
Norway, 42
NRS, viii, 2, 4, 9, 10, 11, 17, 36, 55, 63, 64, 65, 66, 67, 68, 69, 70, 73, 91

O

offenders, 19, 94
Office of National Drug Control Policy (ONDCP), 3, 4, 5, 34, 73
officials, vii, 1, 2, 3, 5, 6, 9, 12, 13, 14, 15, 16, 18, 19, 20, 21, 22, 23, 24, 25, 26, 27, 28, 29, 30, 31, 33, 94
OH, 66
Oklahoma, 93
ONDCP, vii, 1, 4, 5, 6, 7, 21, 22, 24, 26, 29, 30, 31, 32, 35
opiates, 44
original training, 25
overtime, 23

P

Pacific, 4, 36, 43, 73
pain, 11, 17, 36
participants, 26, 52, 69
penalties, 77, 83, 93
permit, 68, 94
pharmacokinetics, 78
phlebotomy, 26
physicians, 30, 81, 90
pilot study, 100
placebo, 99
plasma levels, 79
police, 3, 24, 29, 34, 52, 92, 94
policy, 5, 28, 58, 68
poor performance, 18
population, viii, 12, 14, 39, 40, 42, 50, 68, 82, 89
population density, 68
Portugal, 42
positive relationship, 46
predictive validity, 24
preparation, 46, 59
prescription drugs, 30, 80, 88
prevalence rate, 54
prevention, viii, 29, 75, 76
probability, 46, 70
Problem-Specific Guides, 25
professionals, 3, 20, 25, 30, 31, 90
project, 60, 69
protection, 52
psychoactive drug, 70, 78, 79
psychomotor skills, viii, 39
public awareness, 2, 3, 20, 21, 29, 30, 31, 32
public education, 29
public health, 34, 58
public safety, 58
public service, 29
Puerto Rico, 93, 94
punishment, 26

R

race, 47
radio, 29
reaction time, 59, 88, 90
recidivism, 26
recognition, 76
recommendations, ix, 6, 22, 34, 76, 77, 84, 96, 97, 99
recreational, viii, 6, 7, 11, 34, 36, 39, 54, 58, 66, 68
regression, 46, 47, 49
regression analysis, 49
reliability, 84, 90
requirements, 14, 19, 24, 30, 87, 95
researchers, 69
resources, 19, 20, 24, 29, 84
respiration, 8
response, vii, 1, 5, 33, 36, 58, 80
restitution, 94
risk(s), vii, viii, ix, 3, 20, 21, 29, 39, 40, 41, 42, 43, 44, 46, 47, 48, 49, 50, 51, 53, 54, 55, 56, 57, 58, 59, 70, 75, 78, 79, 82, 89, 90, 91, 92, 95
risk-taking, 59

S

Safe, Accountable, Flexible, Efficient Transportation Equity Act A Legacy for Users (SAFETEA-LU), viii, 75, 76
safety, 3, 6, 7, 18, 19, 20, 29, 31, 32, 34, 58, 69, 88, 90, 98, 99
saliva, 8, 89, 94
SAMHSA, 4, 7, 12, 22, 37
sampling error, 36
sanctions, 94, 96, 97
school, 36
science, 37
scope, viii, 6, 17, 22, 25, 39, 58, 88, 95
security, 24
sedative(s), 15, 44, 46, 65, 91
seizure, 8
Senate, vii, 1, 4, 5, 32
sensitivity, 78, 90
sensors, 25
sentencing, 26, 97
service provider, 37
services, 26
showing, 41
side effects, 16
signs, 83, 84, 87, 100
sobriety, 18
society, 7
software, 24
South Dakota, 93
speech, 18
staffing, 23
stakeholders, 30, 31, 34
standardization, 9, 12, 14
state(s), vii, 1, 2, 3, 5, 6, 7, 9, 11, 12, 13, 14, 15, 16, 17, 18, 19, 20, 21, 22, 23, 25, 26, 27, 28, 29, 30, 31, 32, 33, 34, 35, 37, 68, 81, 99
state laws, 28, 33
statutes, 22, 82, 92, 93, 95, 96
stomach, 78
structure, 37
substance abuse, 94
Substance Abuse and Mental Health Services Administration (SAMHSA), 6, 34
supervision, 26
sweat, 85
sweat test, 85
Sweden, 42, 100
symptoms, 18, 27, 83, 84, 87, 100
synergistic effect, 16

T

target, 36
target population, 36
teams, 44, 52
technical assistance, 7, 25
technical comments, 32
technical support, 25
techniques, 23, 69
technology(s), 30, 68, 76, 77, 81, 82, 85, 100
telephone, 26
testing, 2, 3, 9, 11, 14, 15, 17, 19, 22, 23, 25, 30, 31, 36, 37, 40, 46, 68, 70, 79, 83, 84, 85, 88, 90, 93, 100
threshold level, 29, 77, 82
time constraints, 19
time frame, 69
time periods, 69
toxicology, 6, 9, 12, 13, 14, 15, 19, 22, 63, 77, 81, 84, 99
tracks, 12
traffic crashes, vii, ix, 1, 5, 37, 58, 75, 77, 95
traffic stops, 12, 13
training, ix, 3, 18, 23, 24, 25, 26, 30, 31, 75, 76, 81, 84, 87, 95, 99
transportation, 7, 52
treatment, 26, 94

U

uniform, 14

United, v, vii, viii, 1, 2, 4, 5, 9, 12, 15, 17, 32, 33, 35, 36, 37, 39, 43, 57, 61, 63, 68, 69, 72, 73, 77, 86, 91
United Nations, 17, 37
United States, v, vii, viii, 1, 2, 4, 5, 9, 12, 15, 17, 32, 33, 35, 36, 39, 43, 57, 61, 63, 68, 69, 72, 73, 77, 86, 91
universe, 18
urinalysis, 85
urine, 8, 19, 22, 27, 41, 83, 84, 85, 94

V

validation, 23, 31
variables, 46, 47, 48, 56, 78, 91
variations, 15, 78, 85
vehicles, 34, 53, 90, 91

W

Washington, 6, 7, 10, 14, 26, 27, 28, 29, 31, 34, 35, 36, 37, 59, 60, 61, 72, 93, 97, 98, 99, 100
wear, 16
White House, 3, 5, 34
Wisconsin, 93
working groups, 31
workplace, 22, 37